COOKIE CUTTERS DESIGNED BY:

About This Design Book

Designed by: Kelley M Likes
Recipe by: Judy Schmitz
Illustrated by: Zerin Likes
Cover Designed by: Mary Barrows

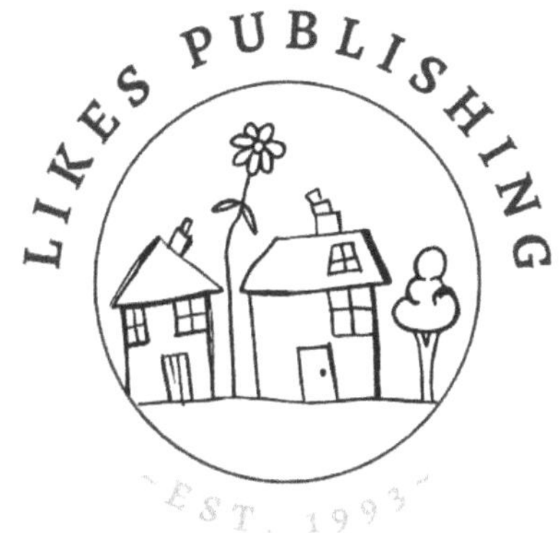

Likes Publishing
Lilburn, GA 30047
Visit us at likespublishing.com

First Edition: January 2024
979-8-88902-035-6
Printed in USA

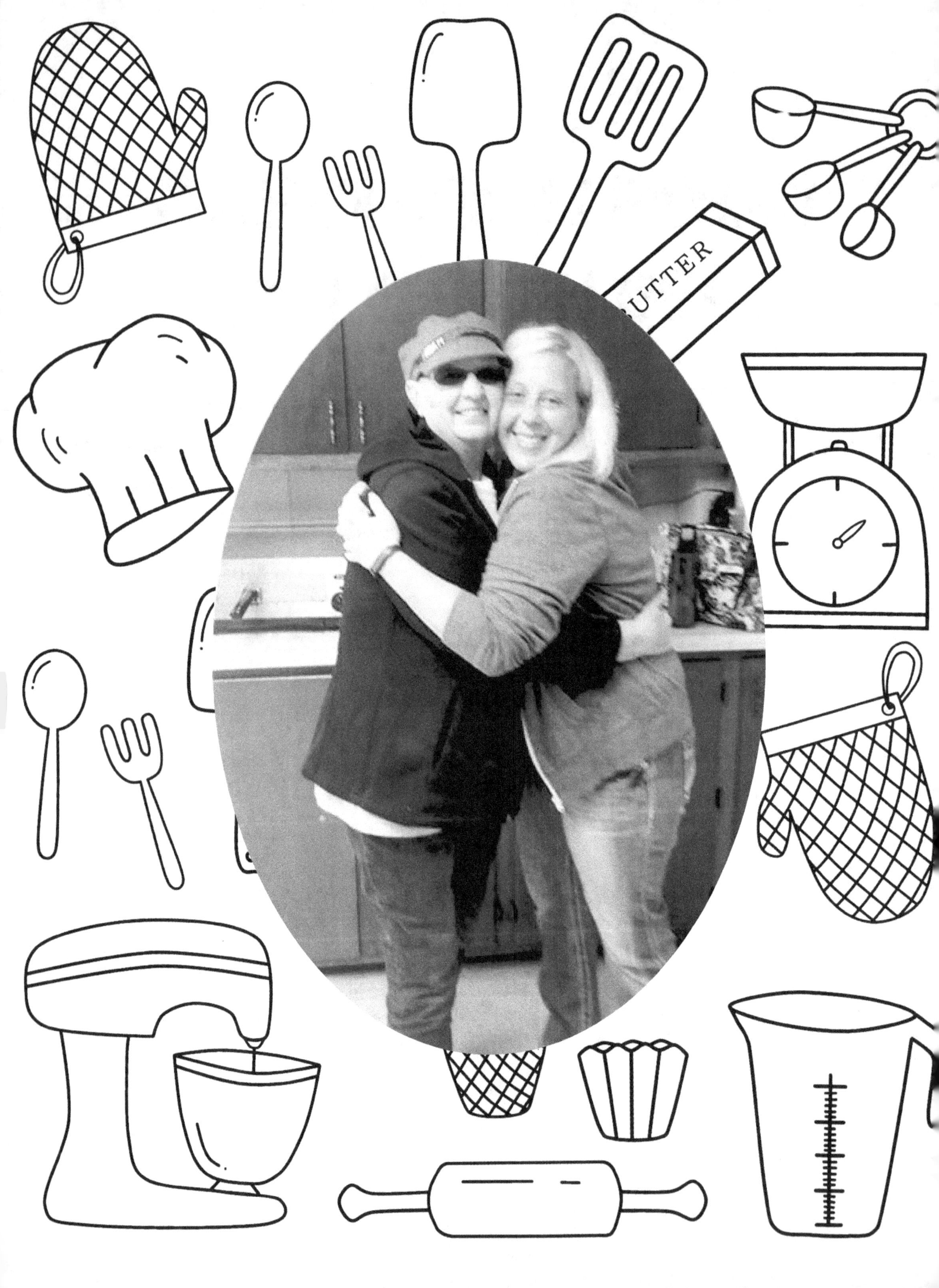

Aunt Judy's Almond Cut-Out Cookies

1. 1 1/2 cups Powedered Sugar

2. 1 cup Butter (softened - room temperature)

3. 1 teaspoon Vanilla

4. 1 Egg

5. 2 1/2 cups All Purpose Flour

6. 1 teaspoon Baking Soda

7. 1/2 teaspoon Almond Extract

8. 1 teaspoon Cream of Tarter

DIRECTIONS:

With a mixer:

Cream together the first 4 ingredients.

Add ingredients 5-8 to the mixture.

Chill for 2 hours in the refridgerator.

Roll out on floured surface.

Fat cookies are soft and chewy. Thin cookies are crunchy.

Cut out cookies using your favorite cookie cutters.

BAKE at 375 degrees for 7-8 minutes.

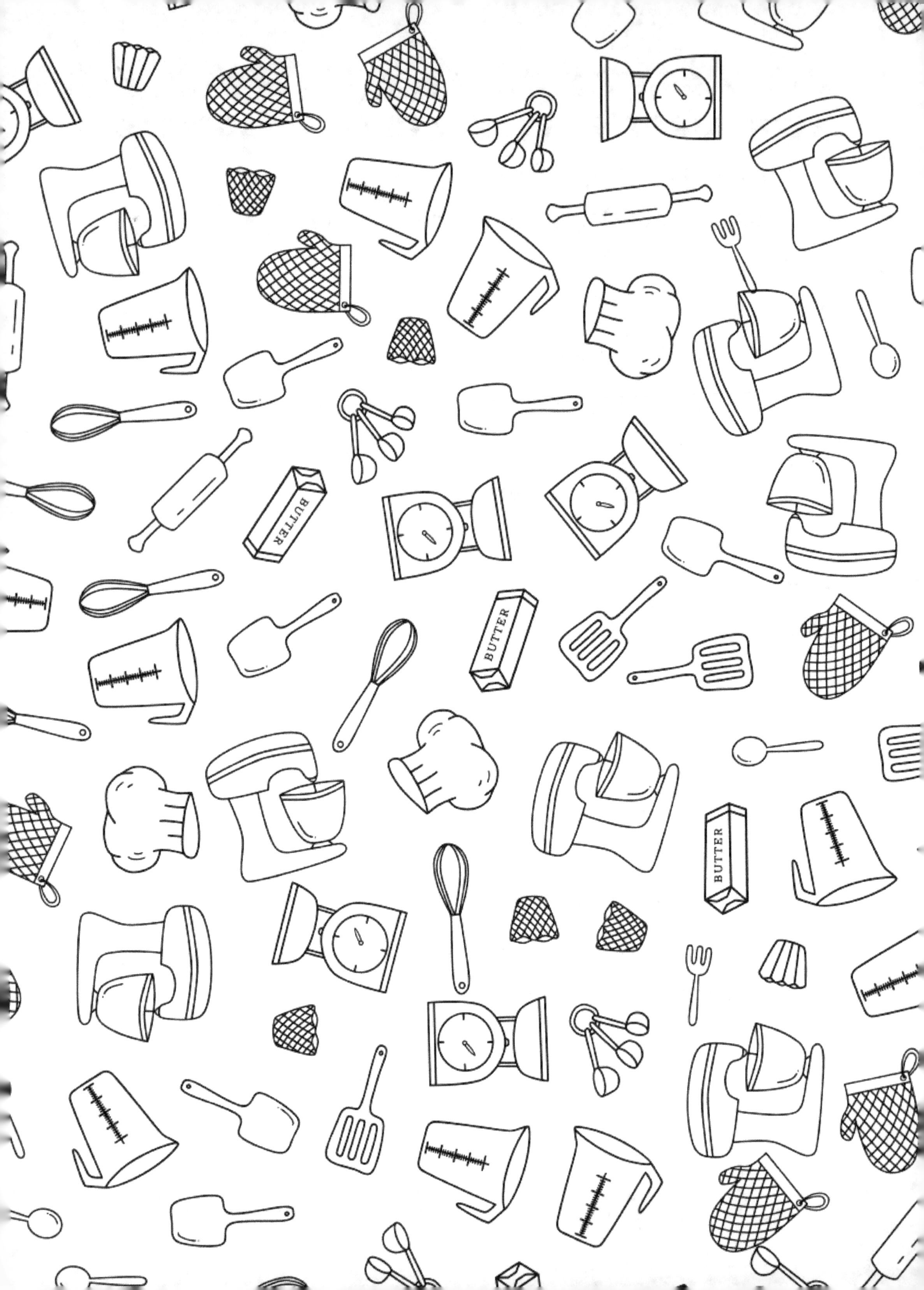

BUTTER
BUTTER
BUTTER

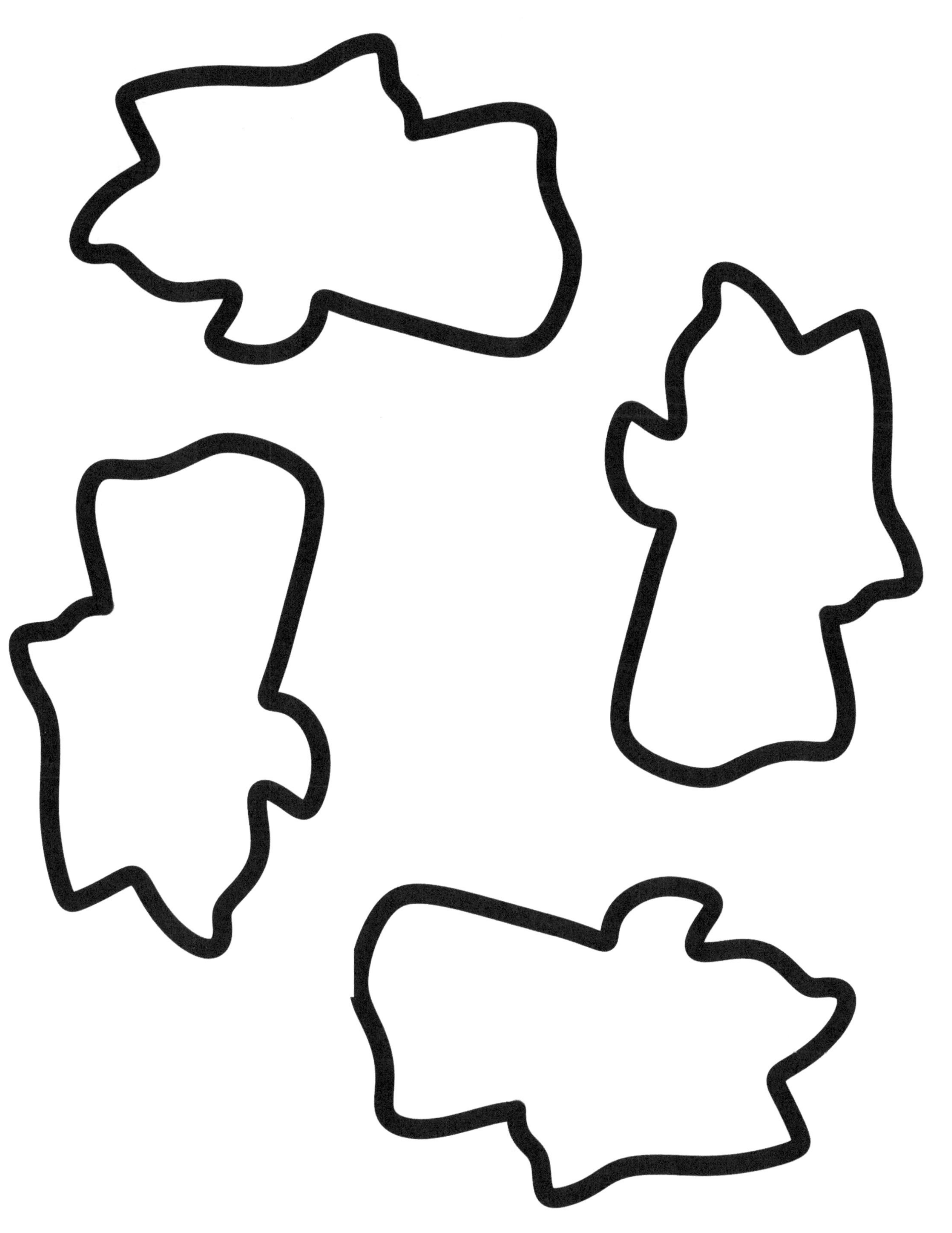

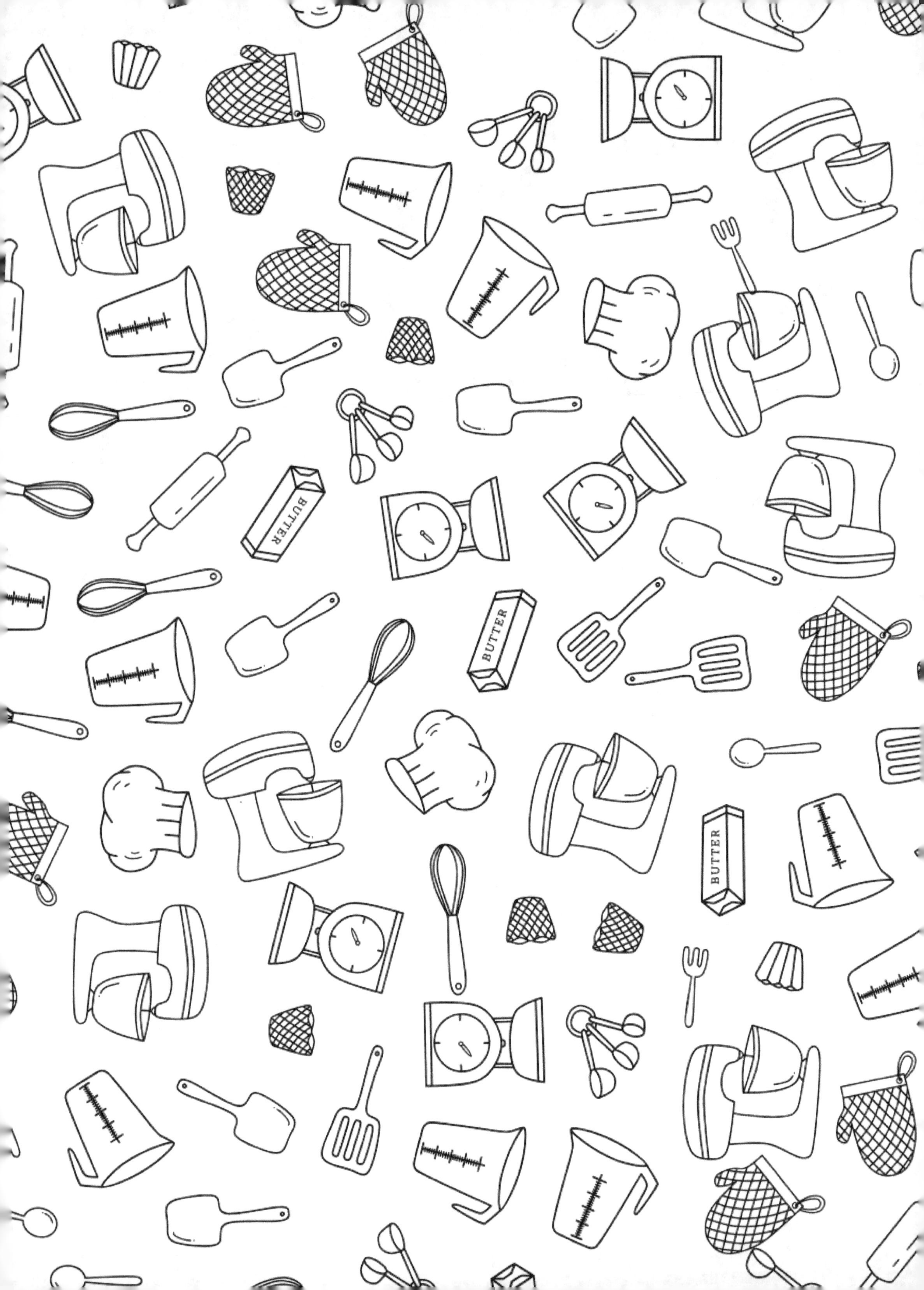

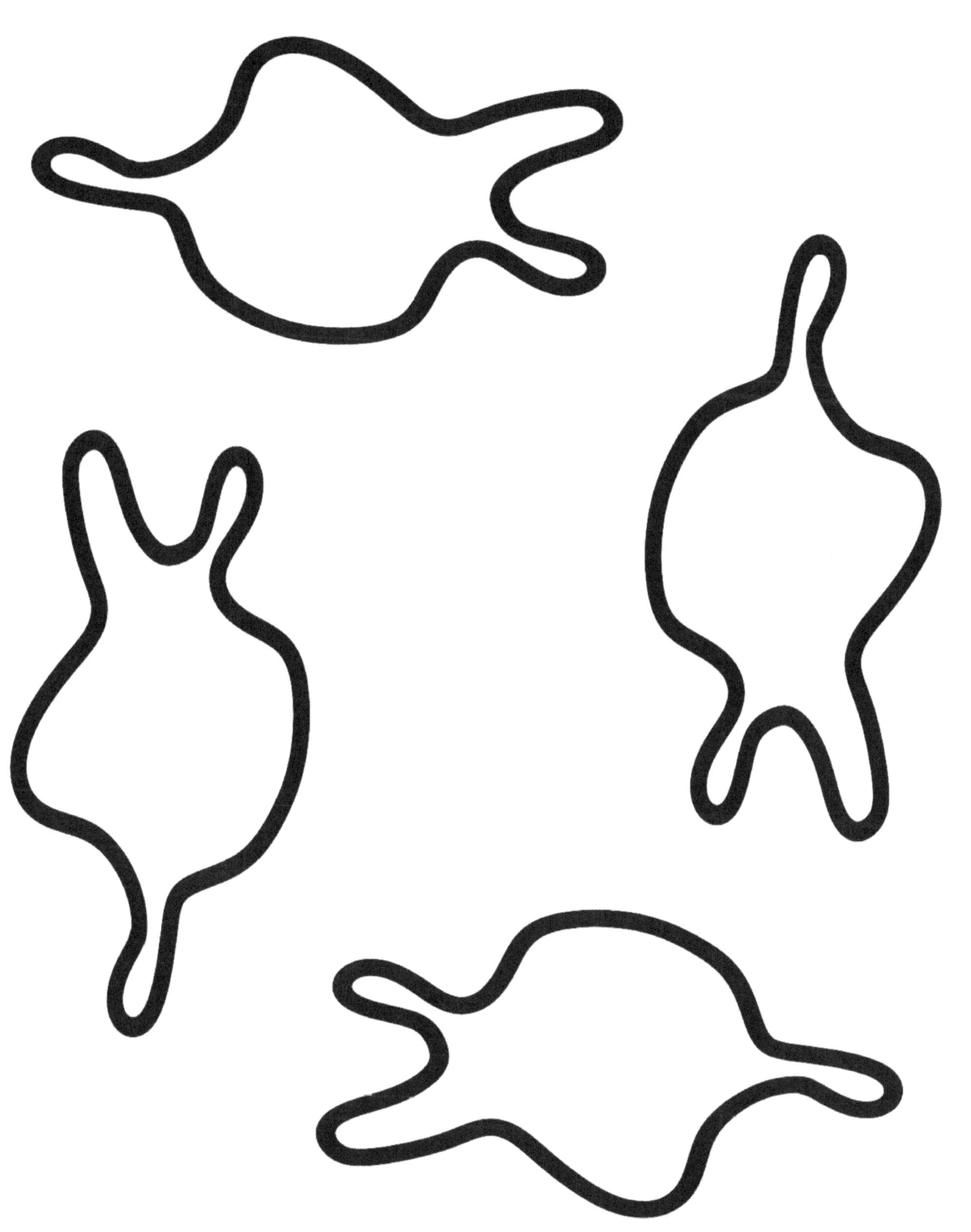

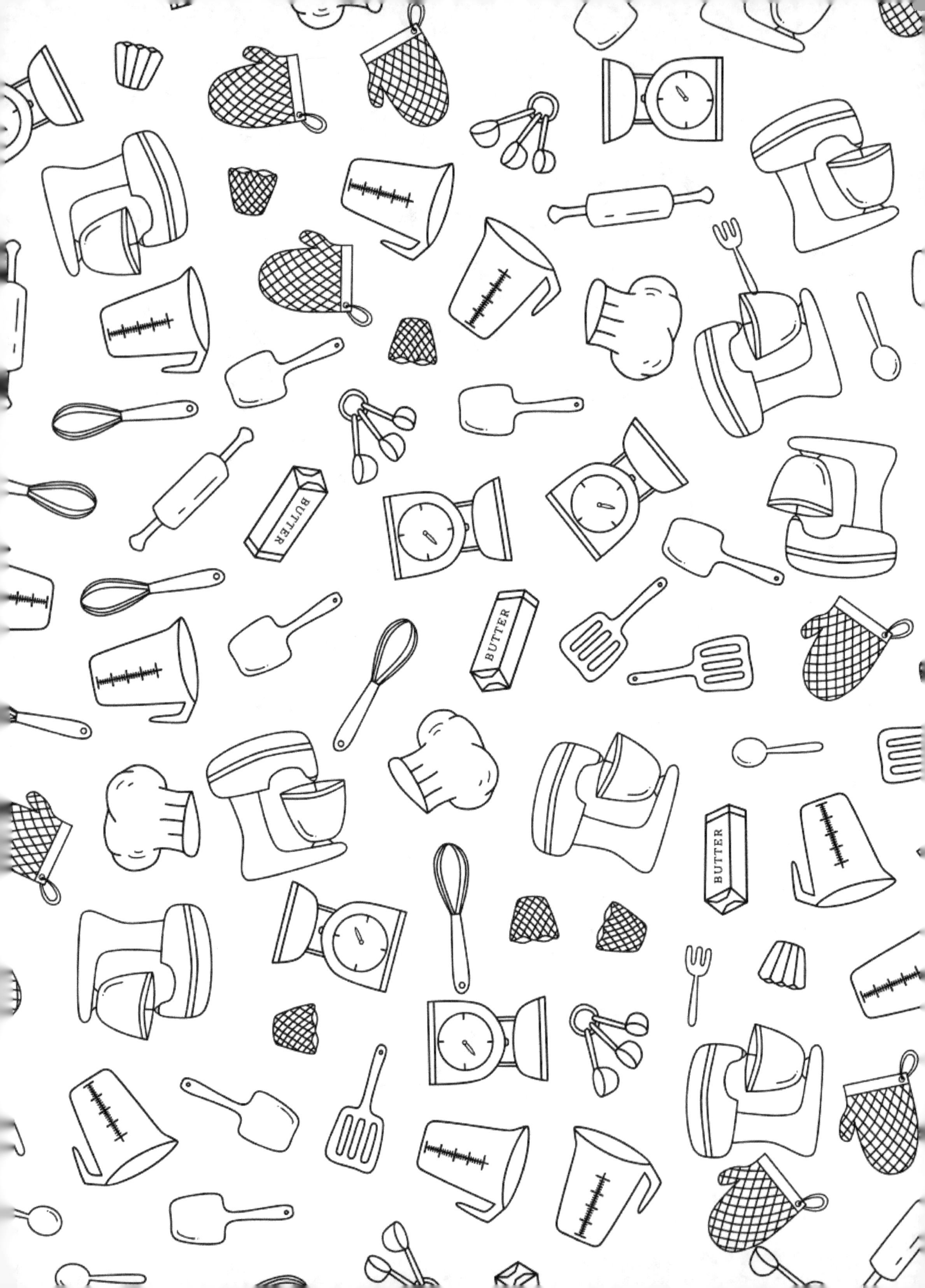

BUTTER
BUTTER
BUTTER

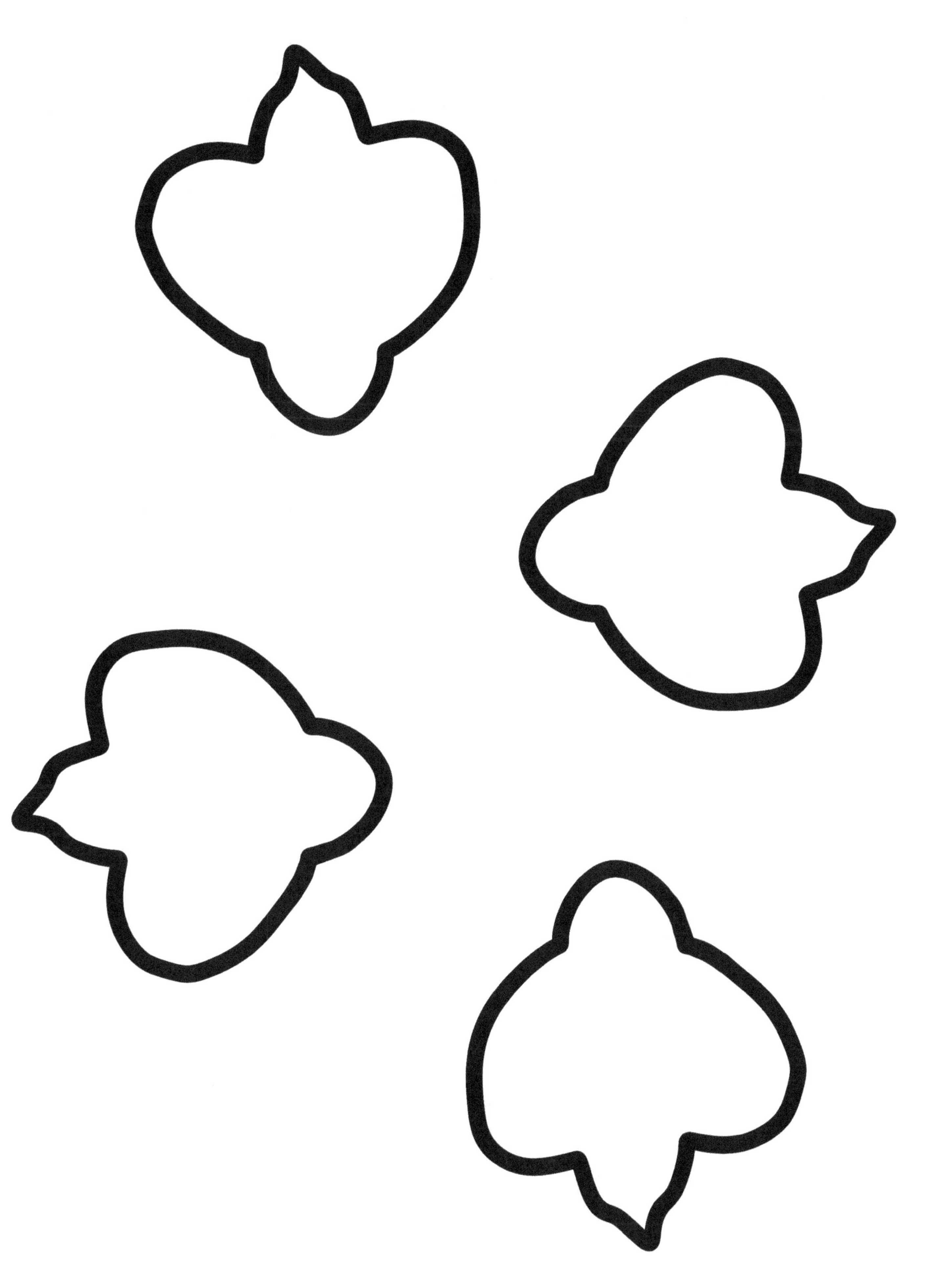

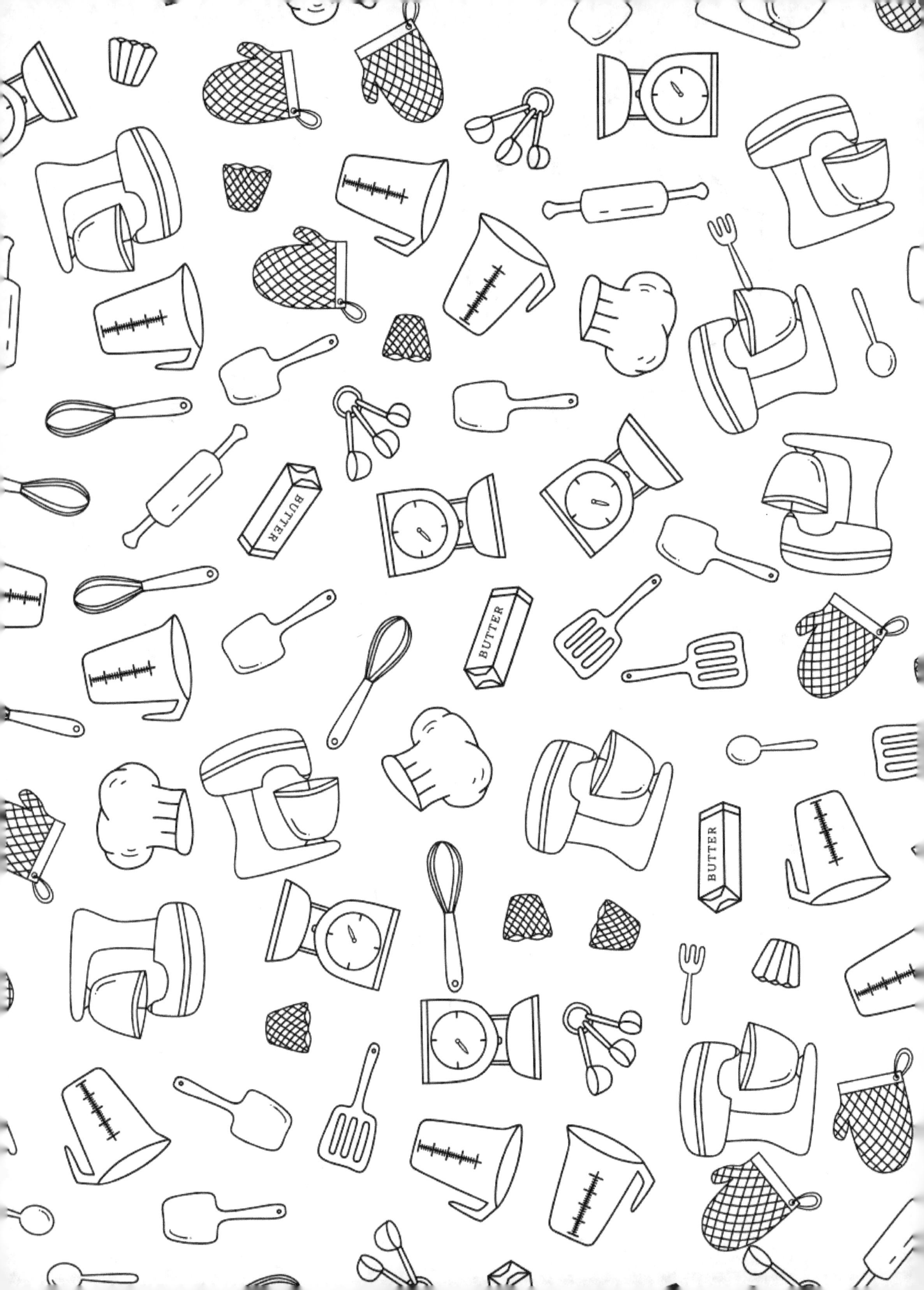

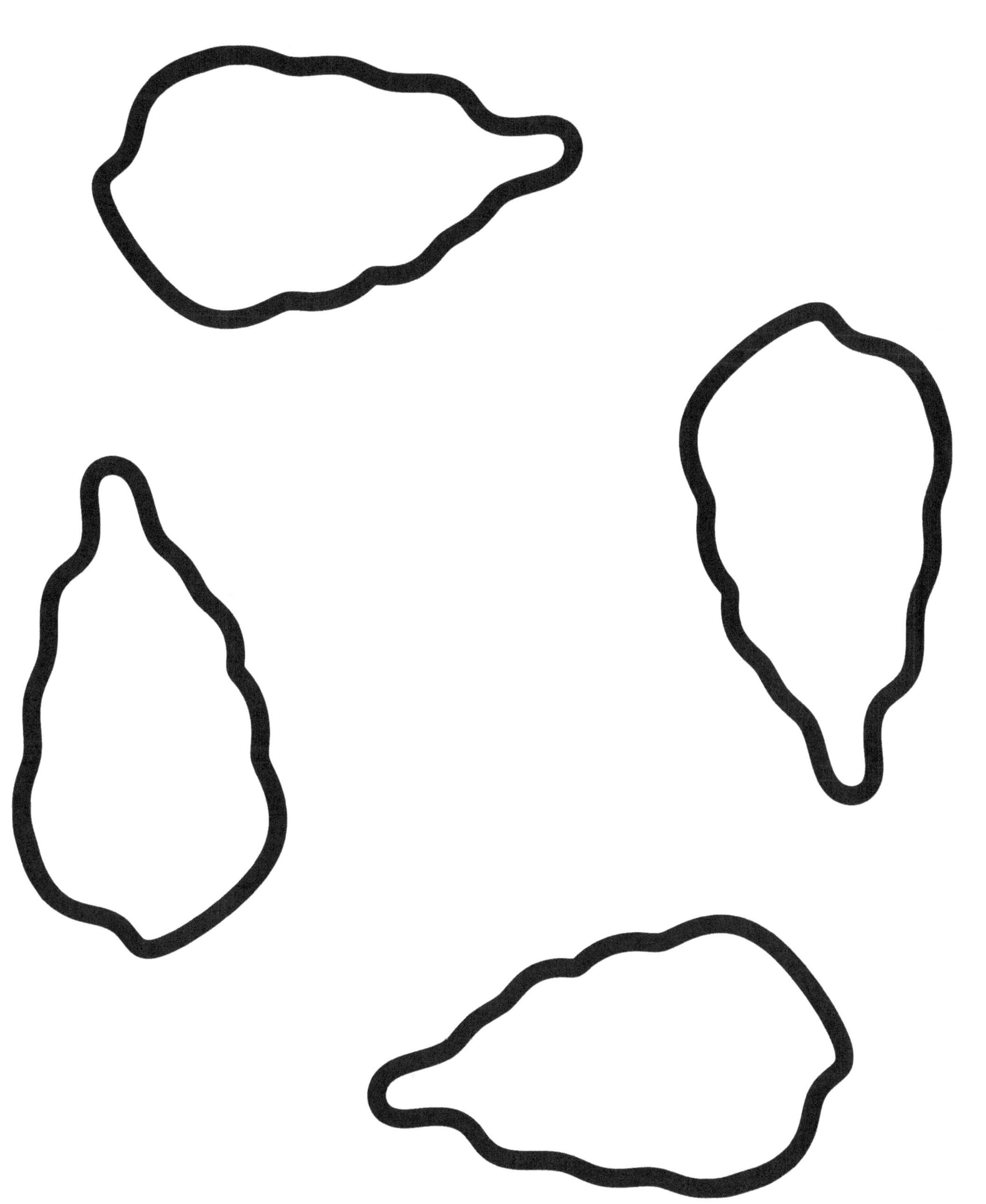

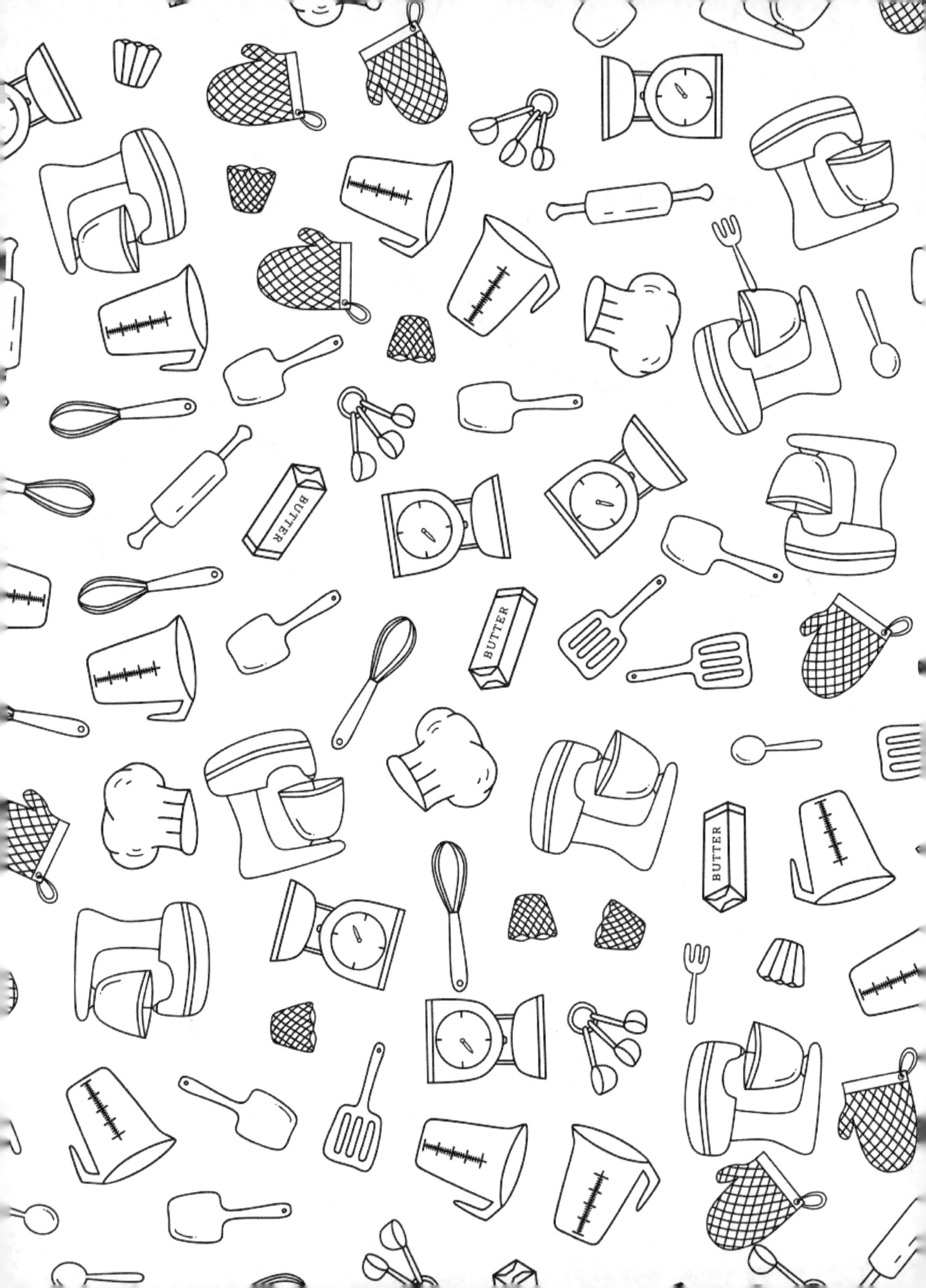

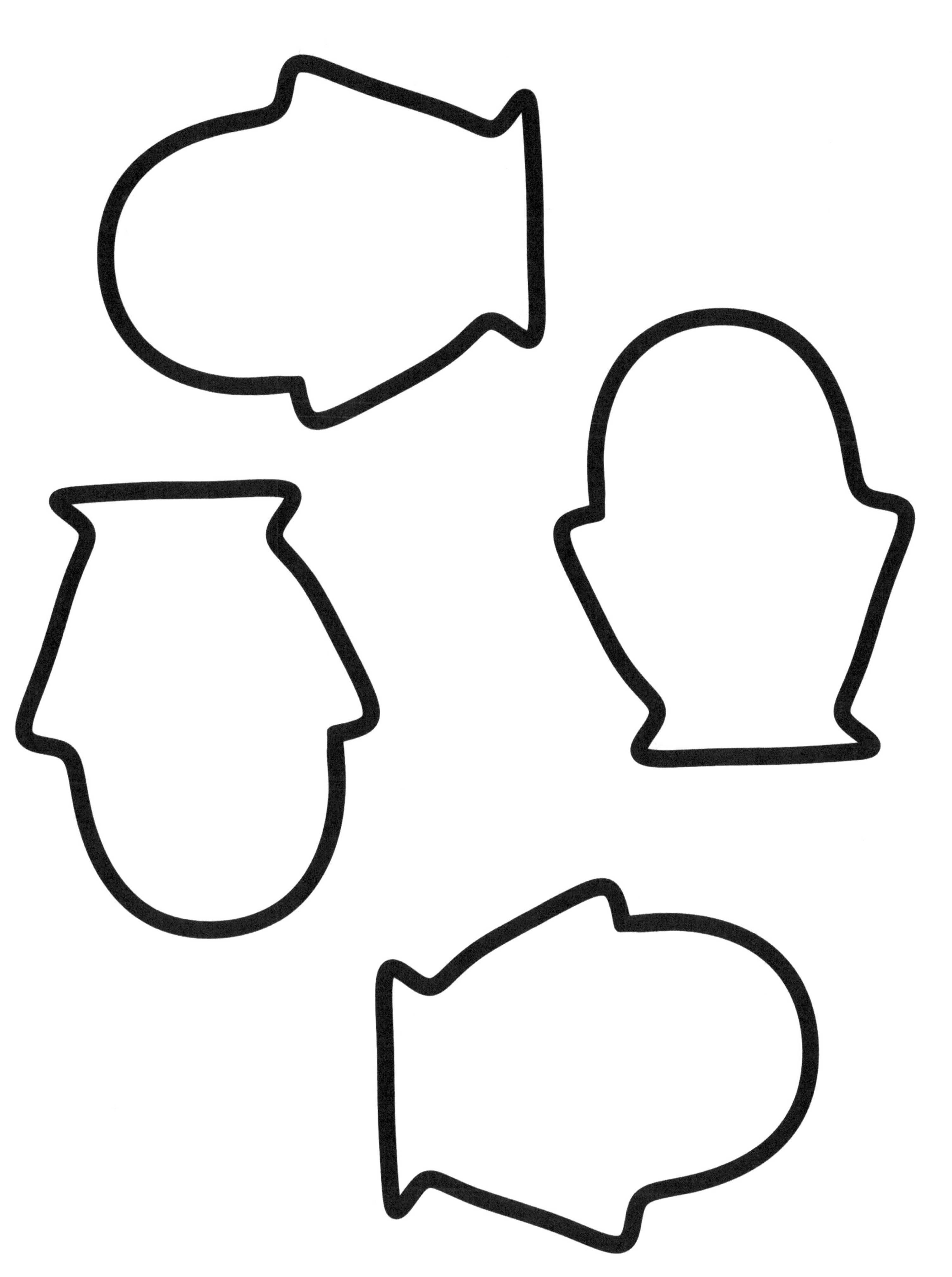

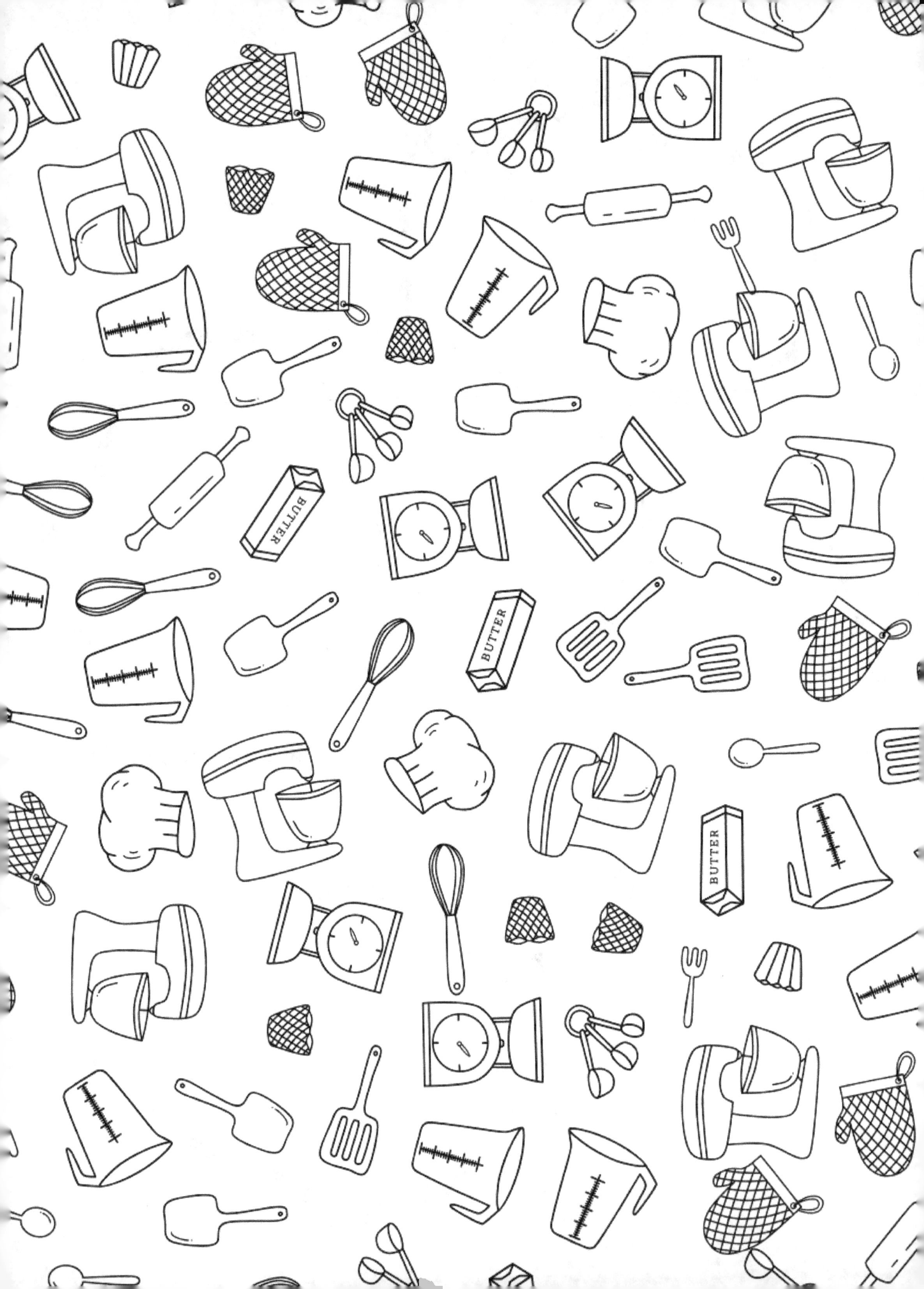

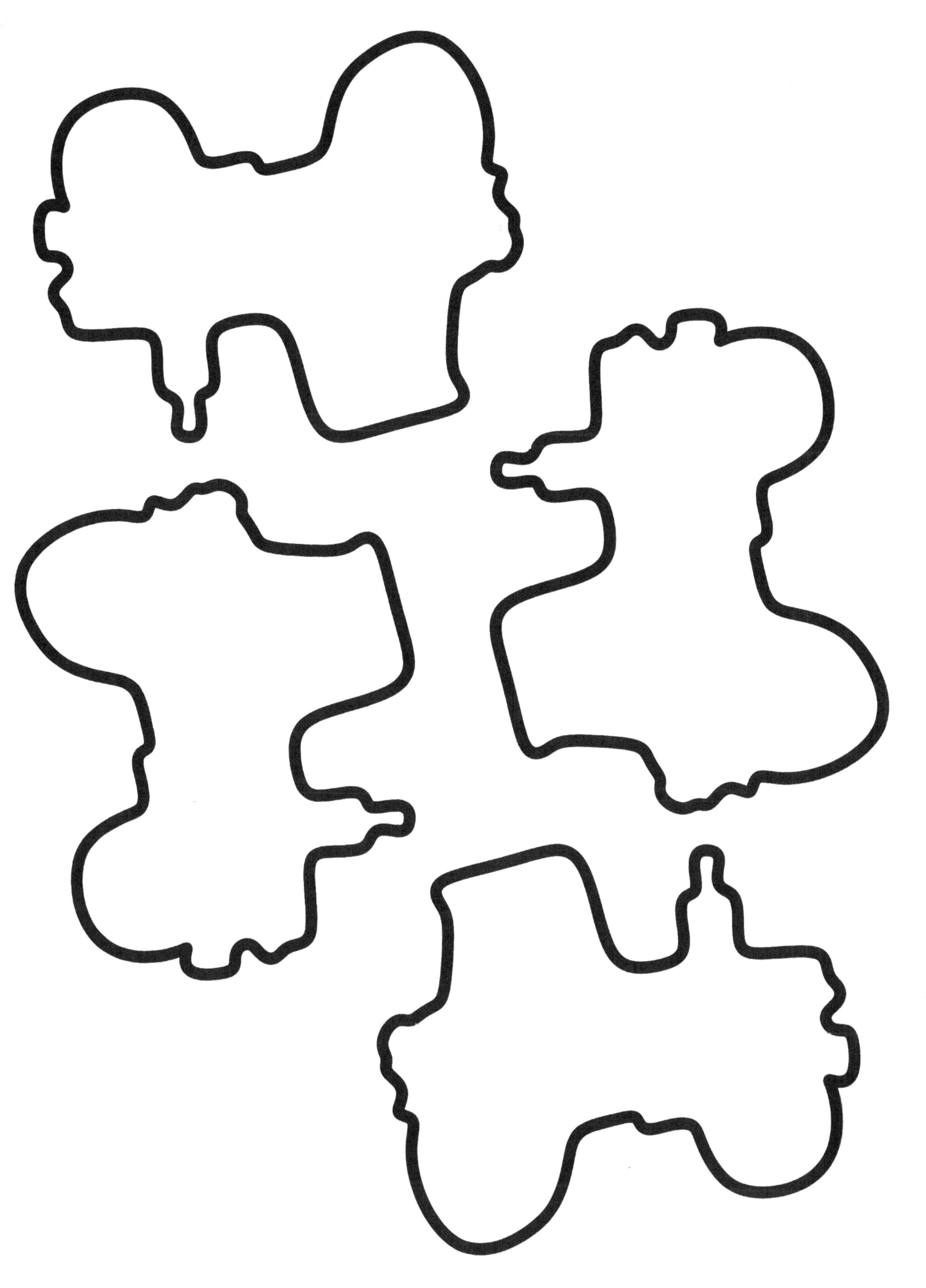

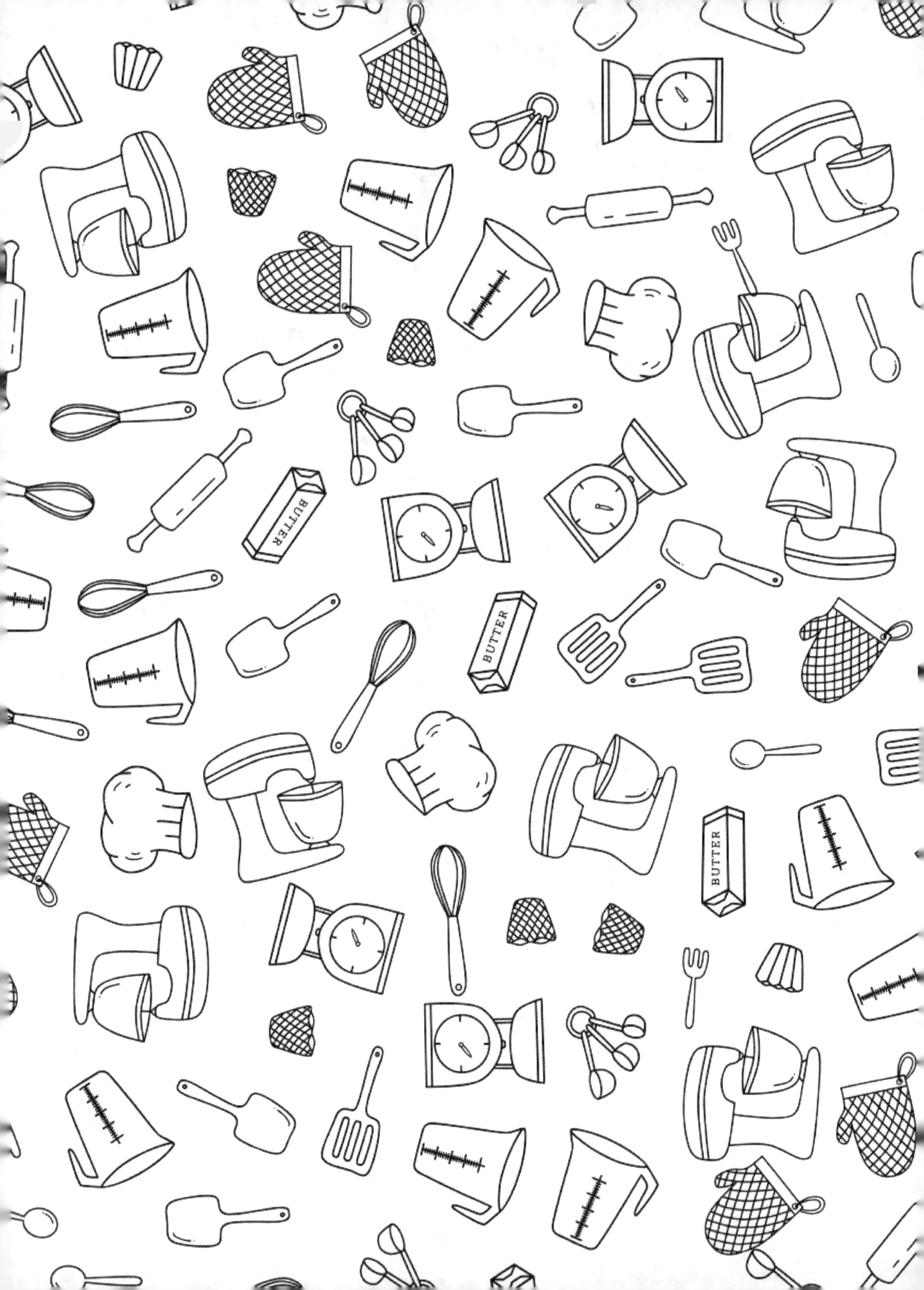

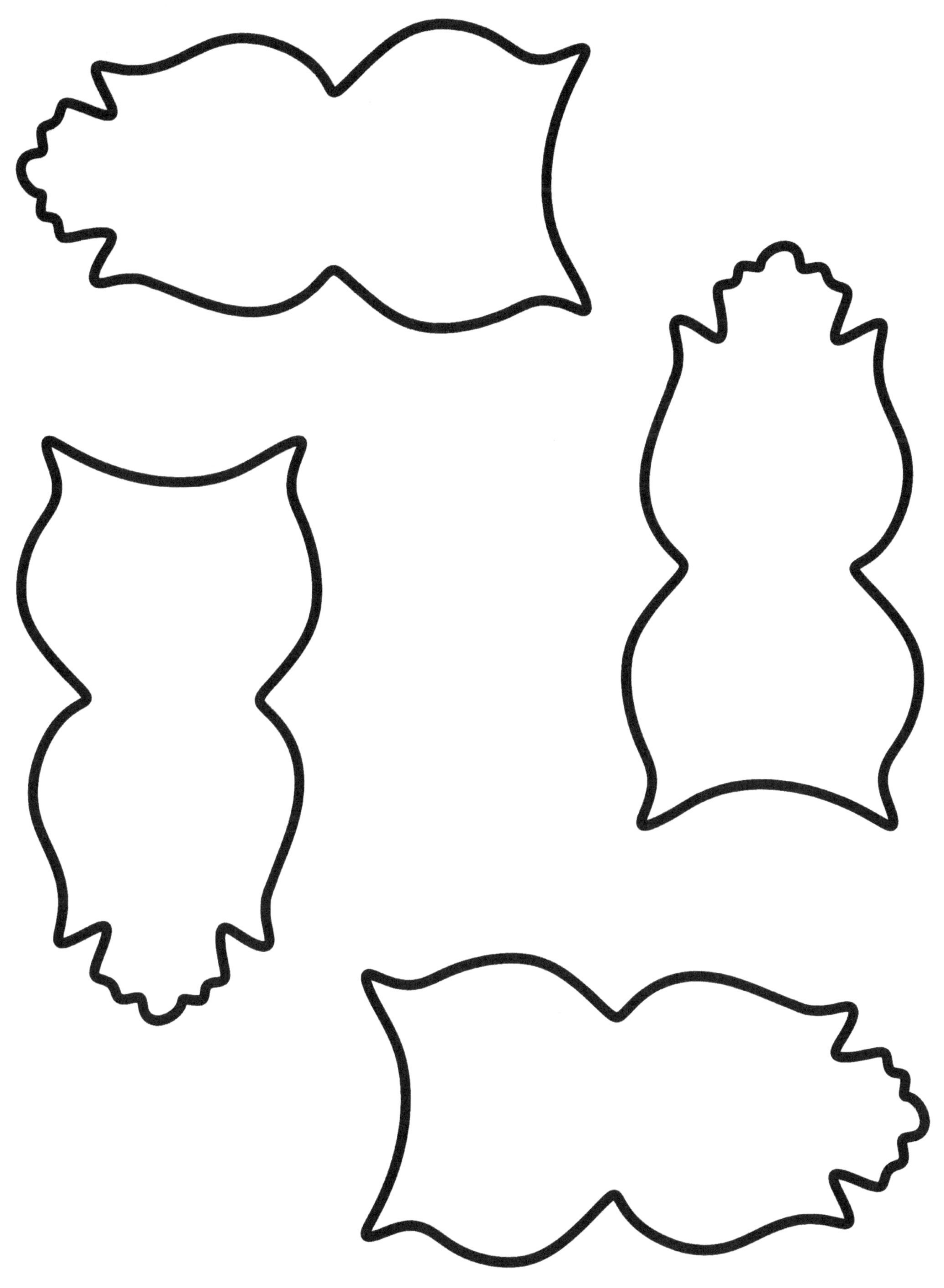

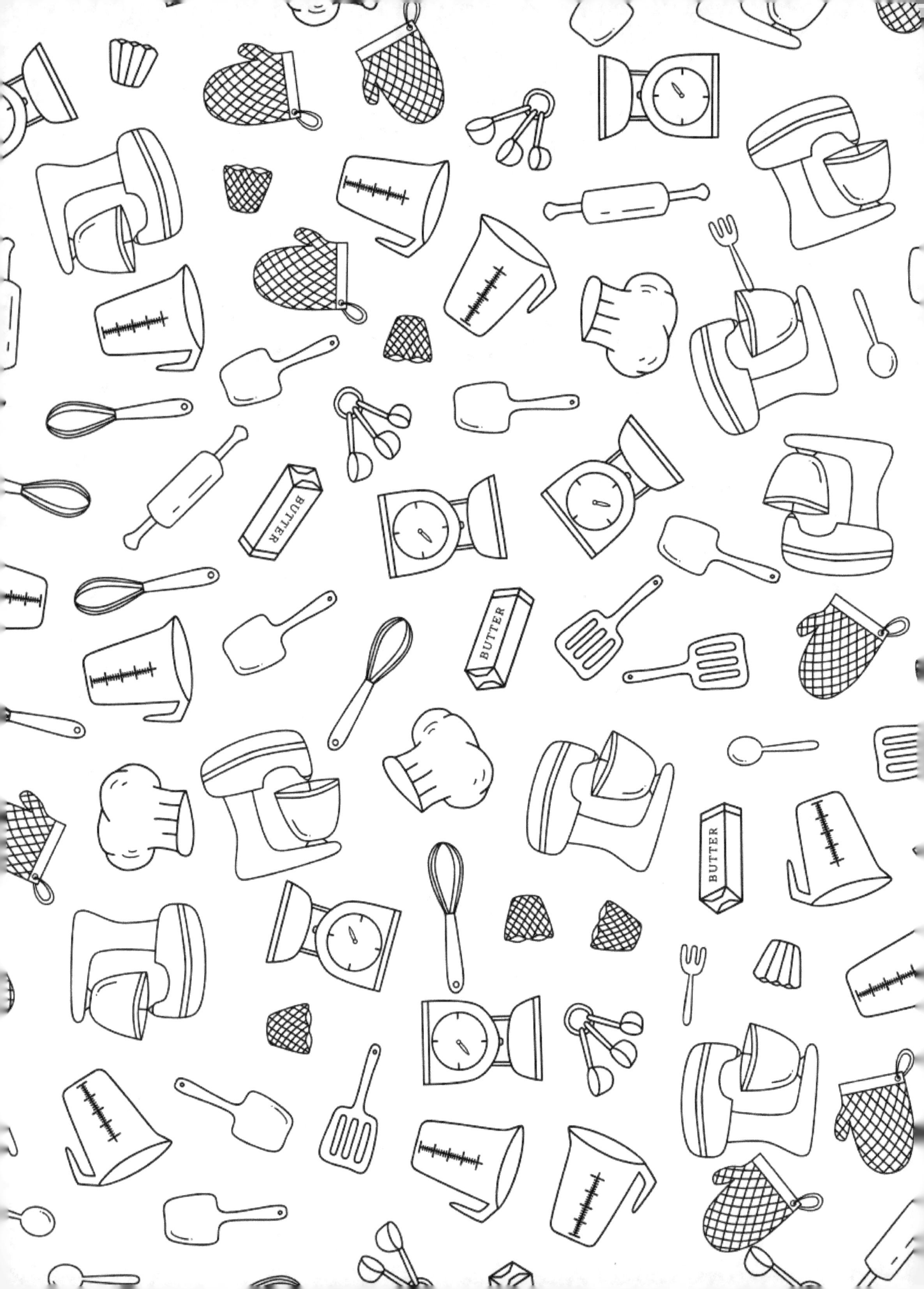

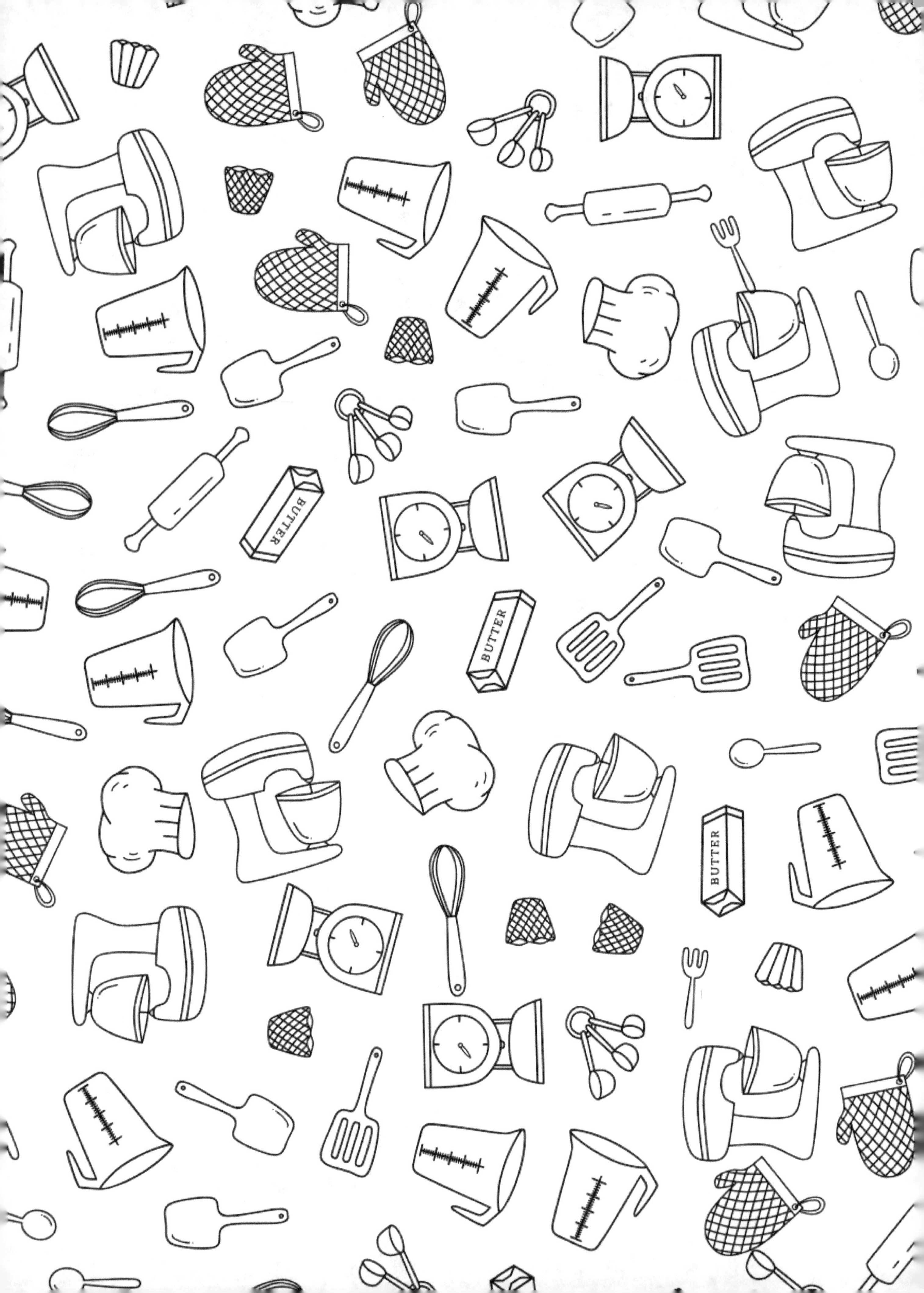

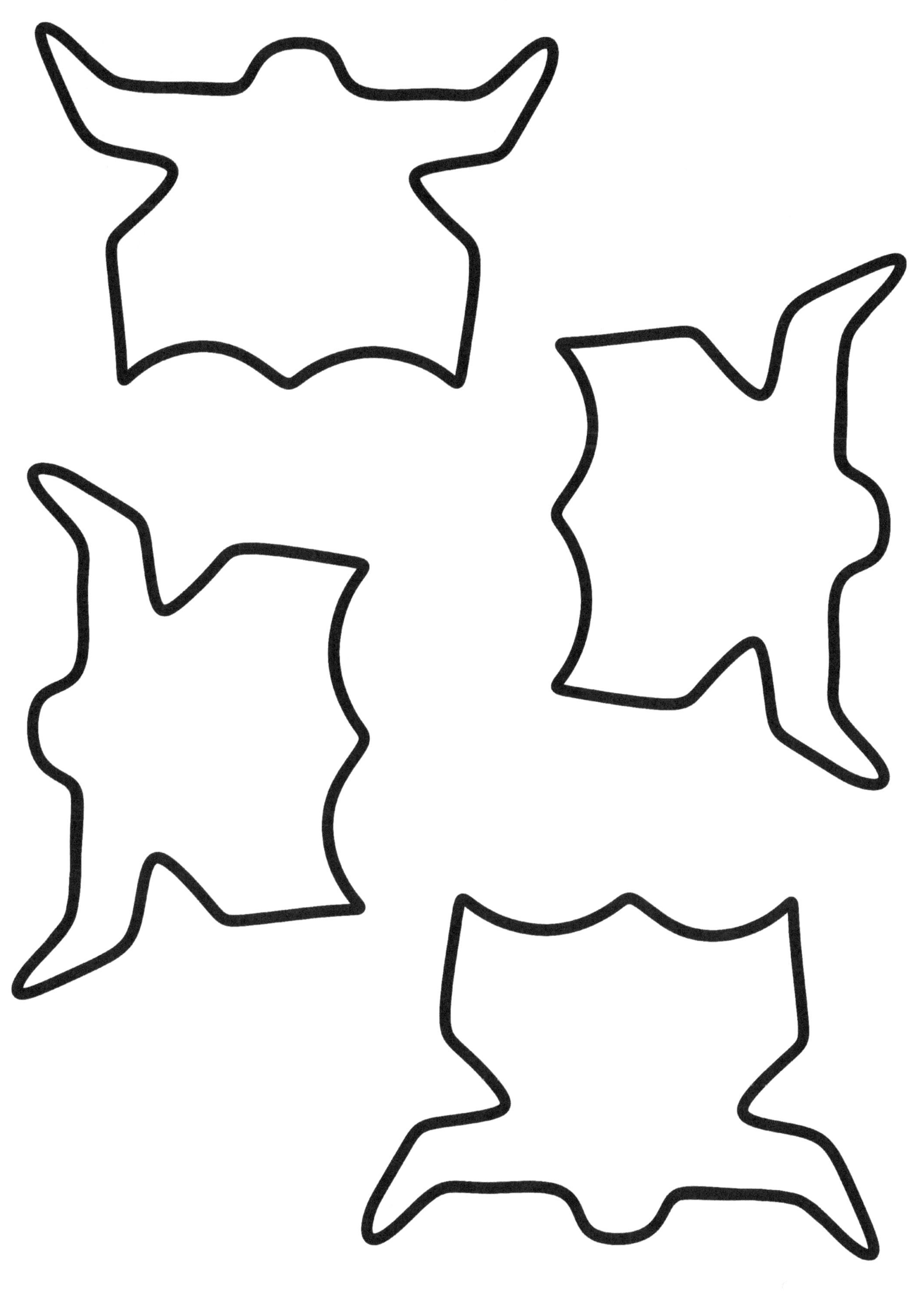

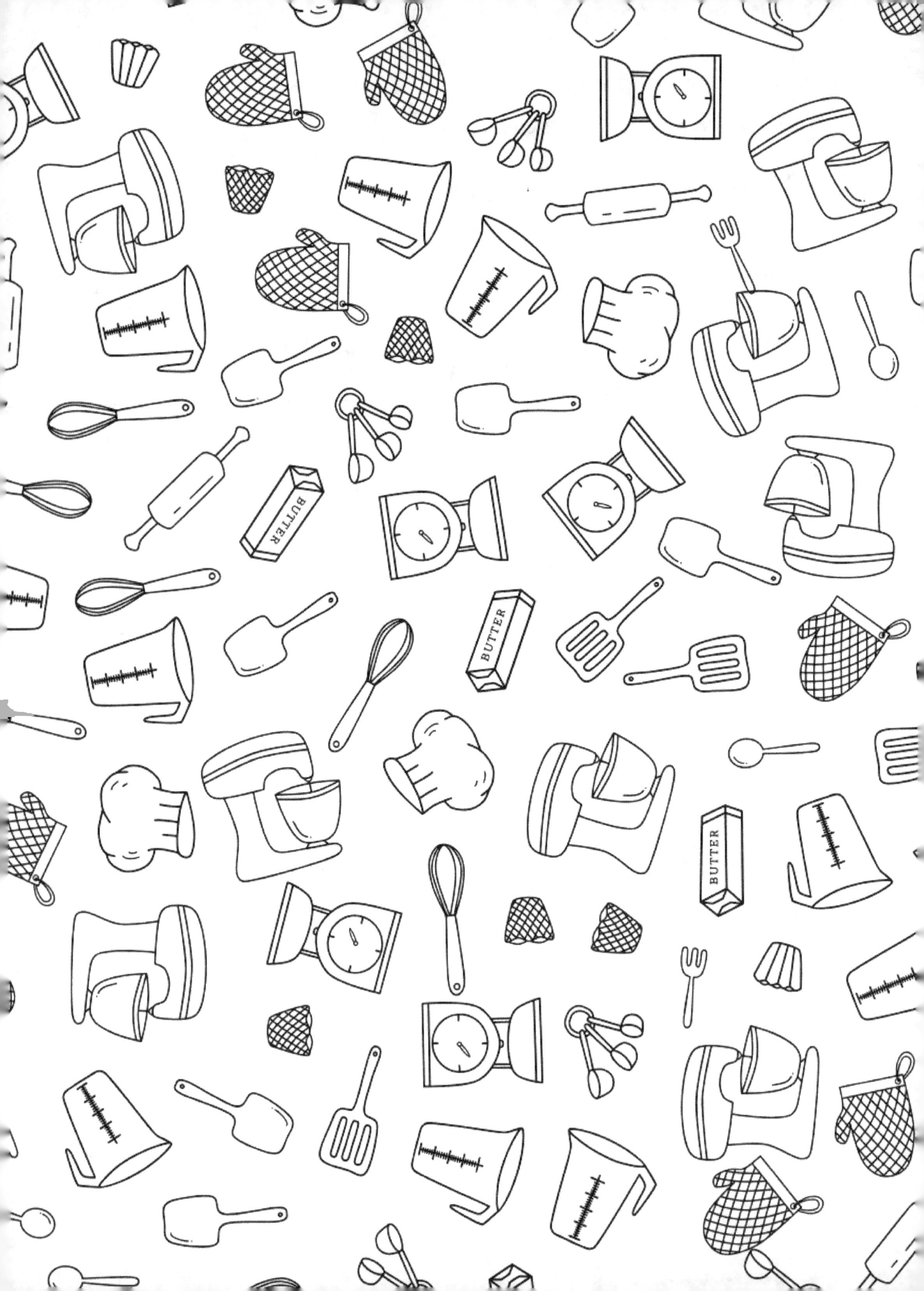
BUTTER
BUTTER
BUTTER
BUTTER

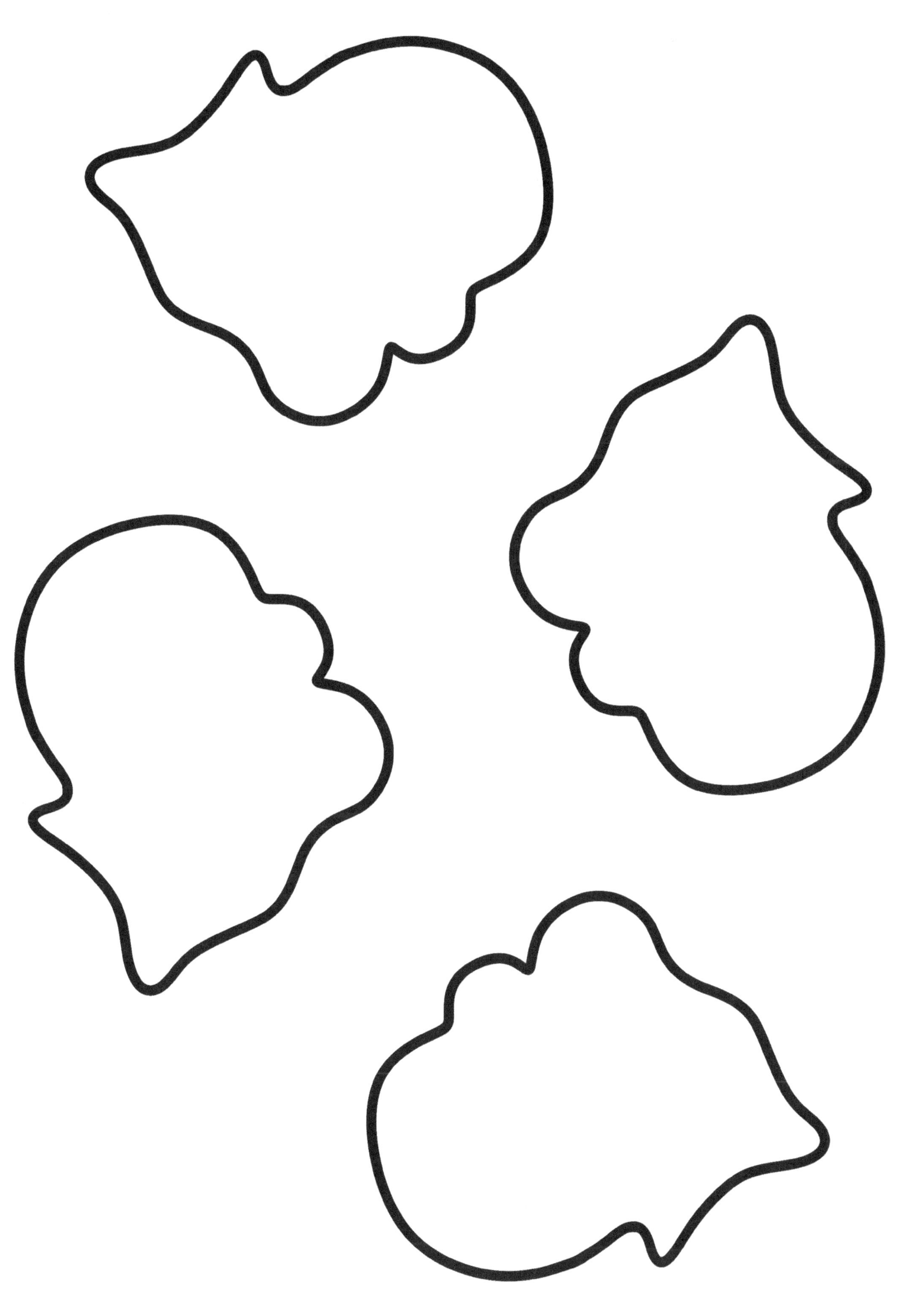

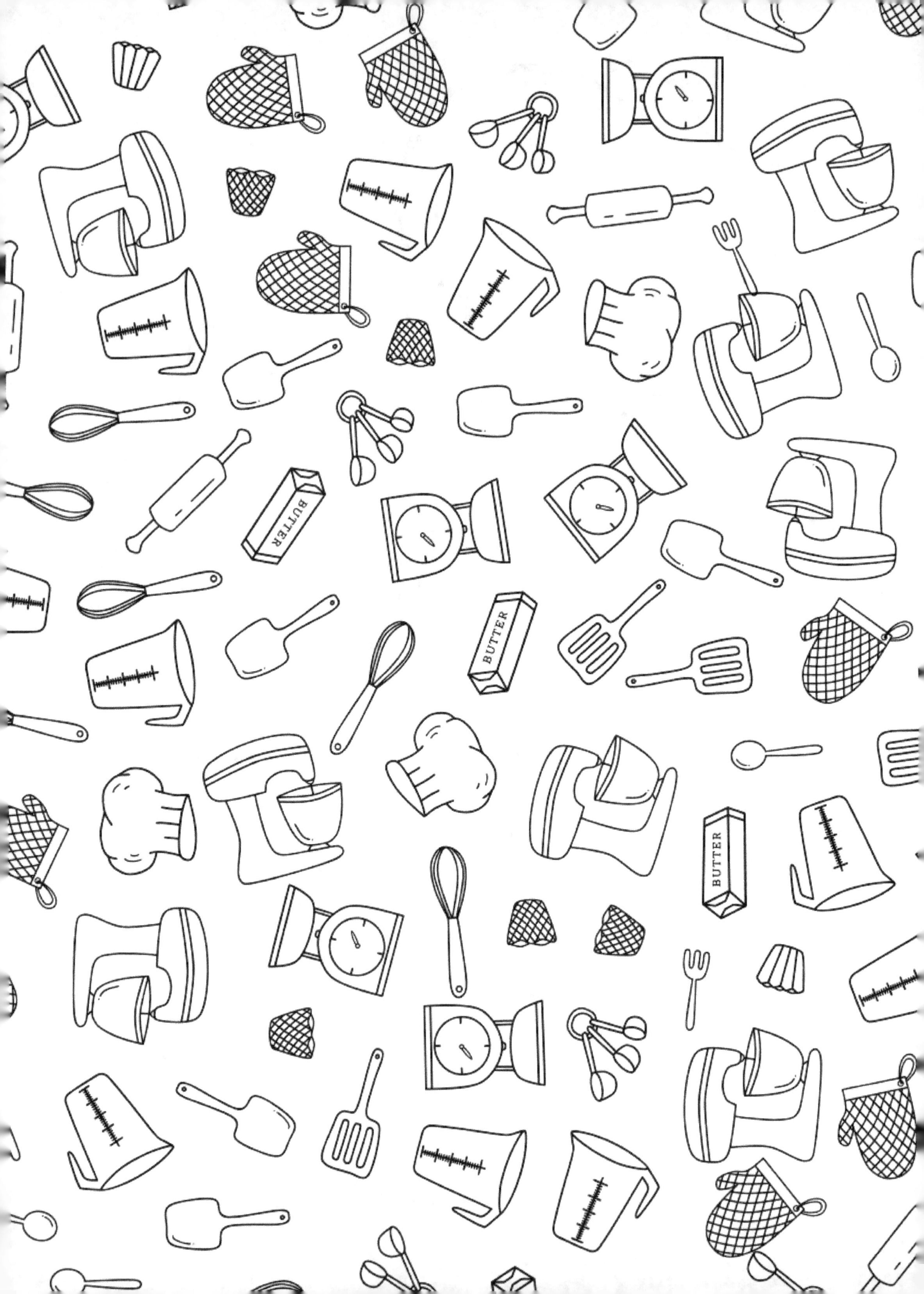

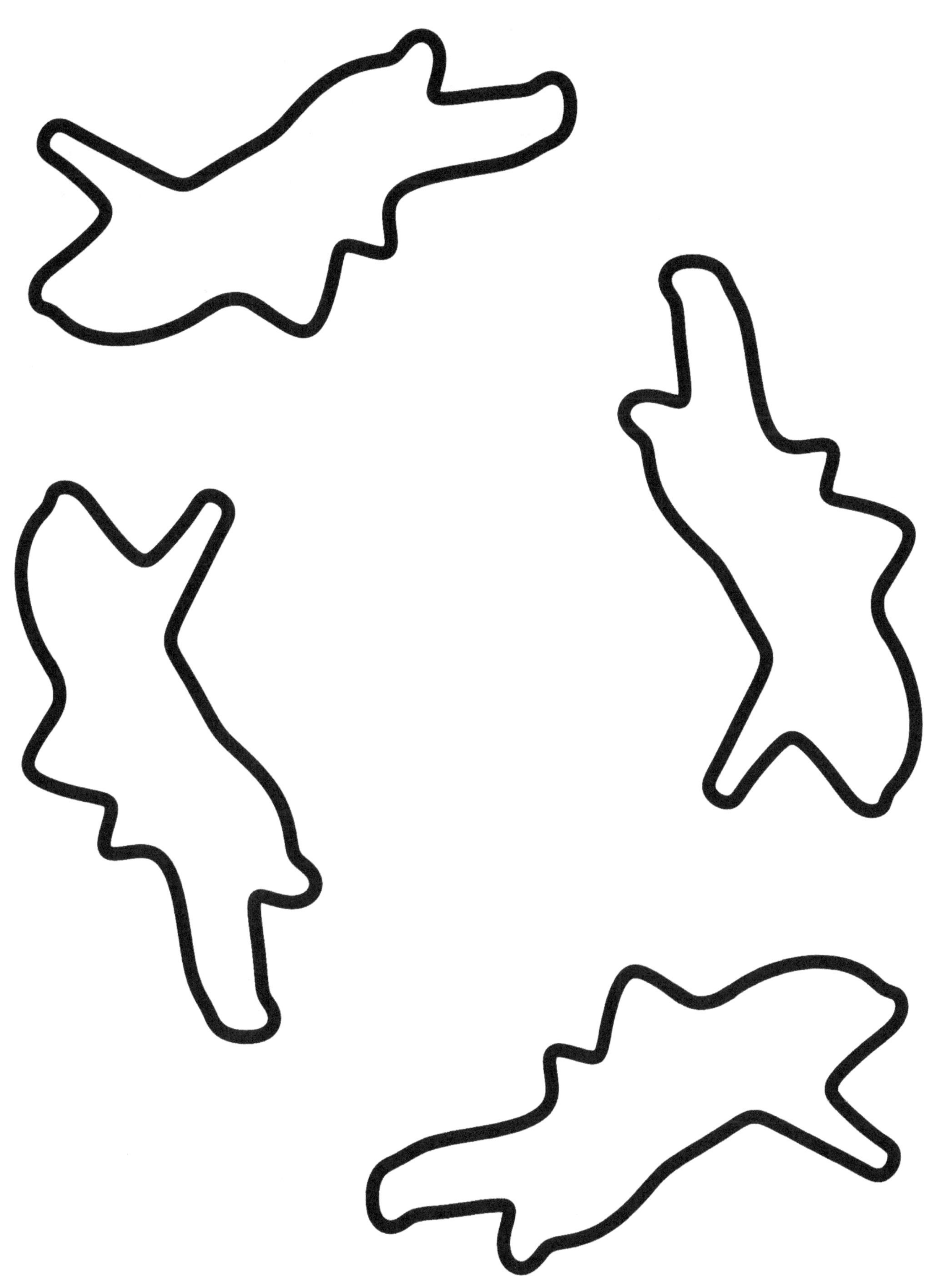

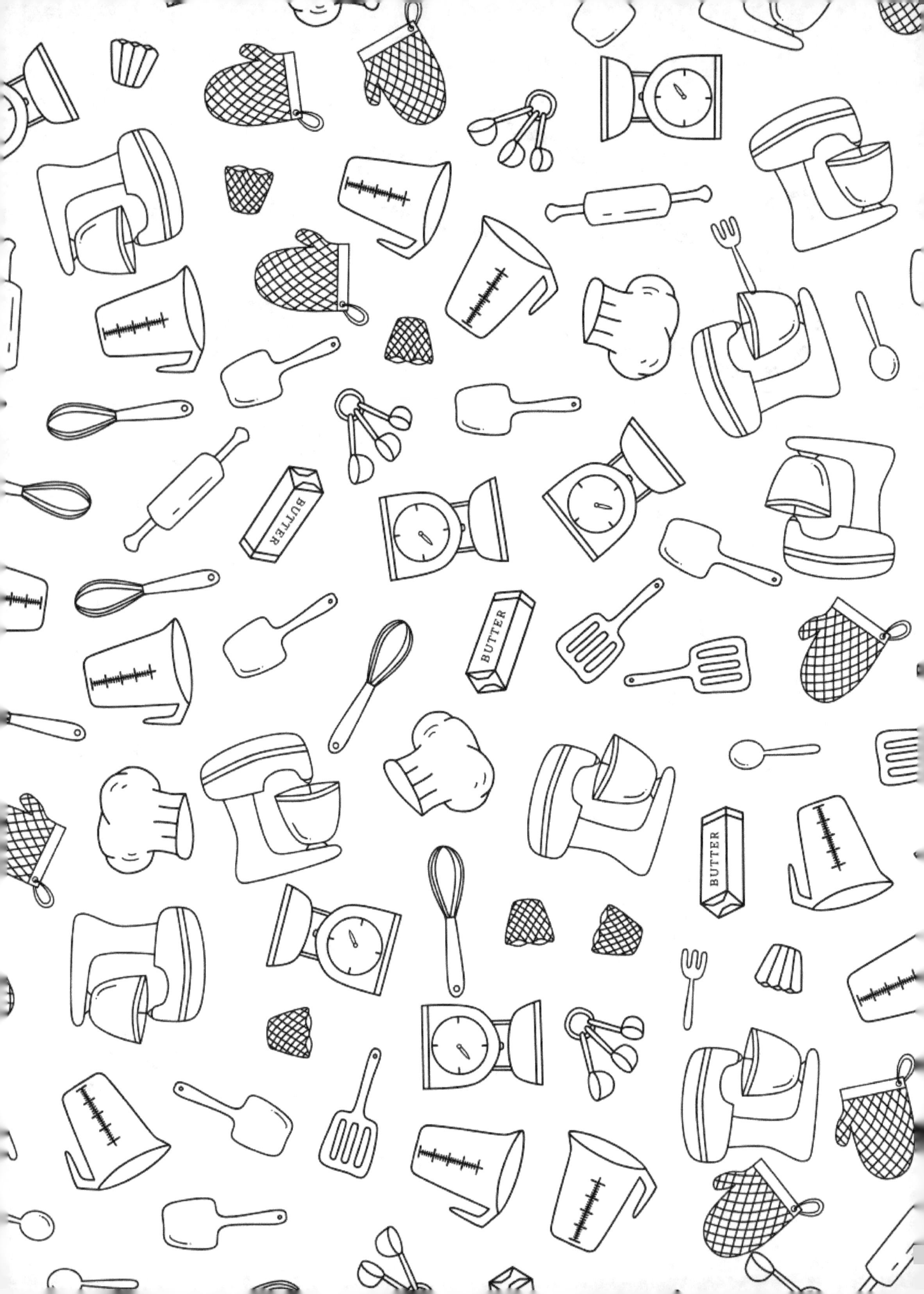

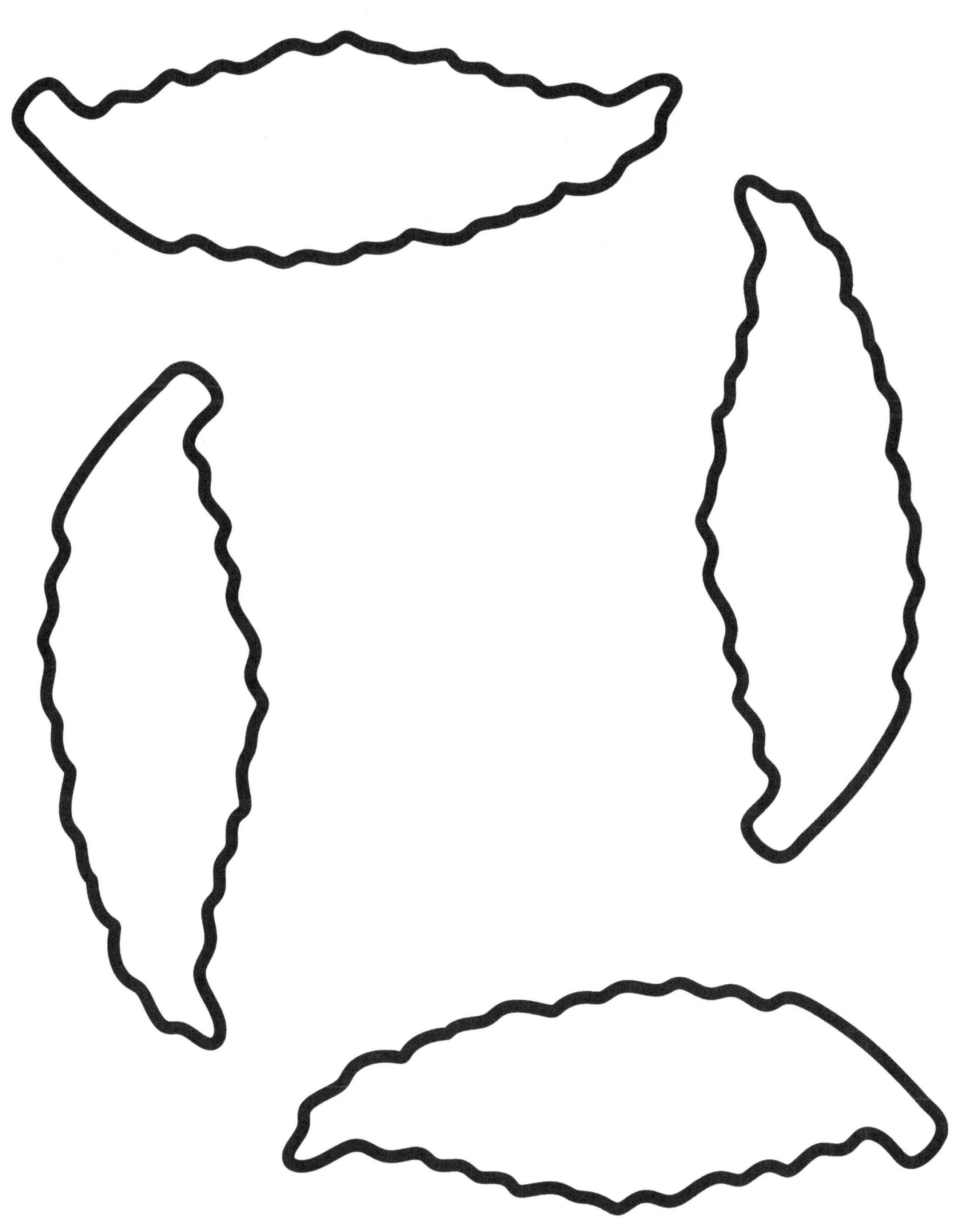

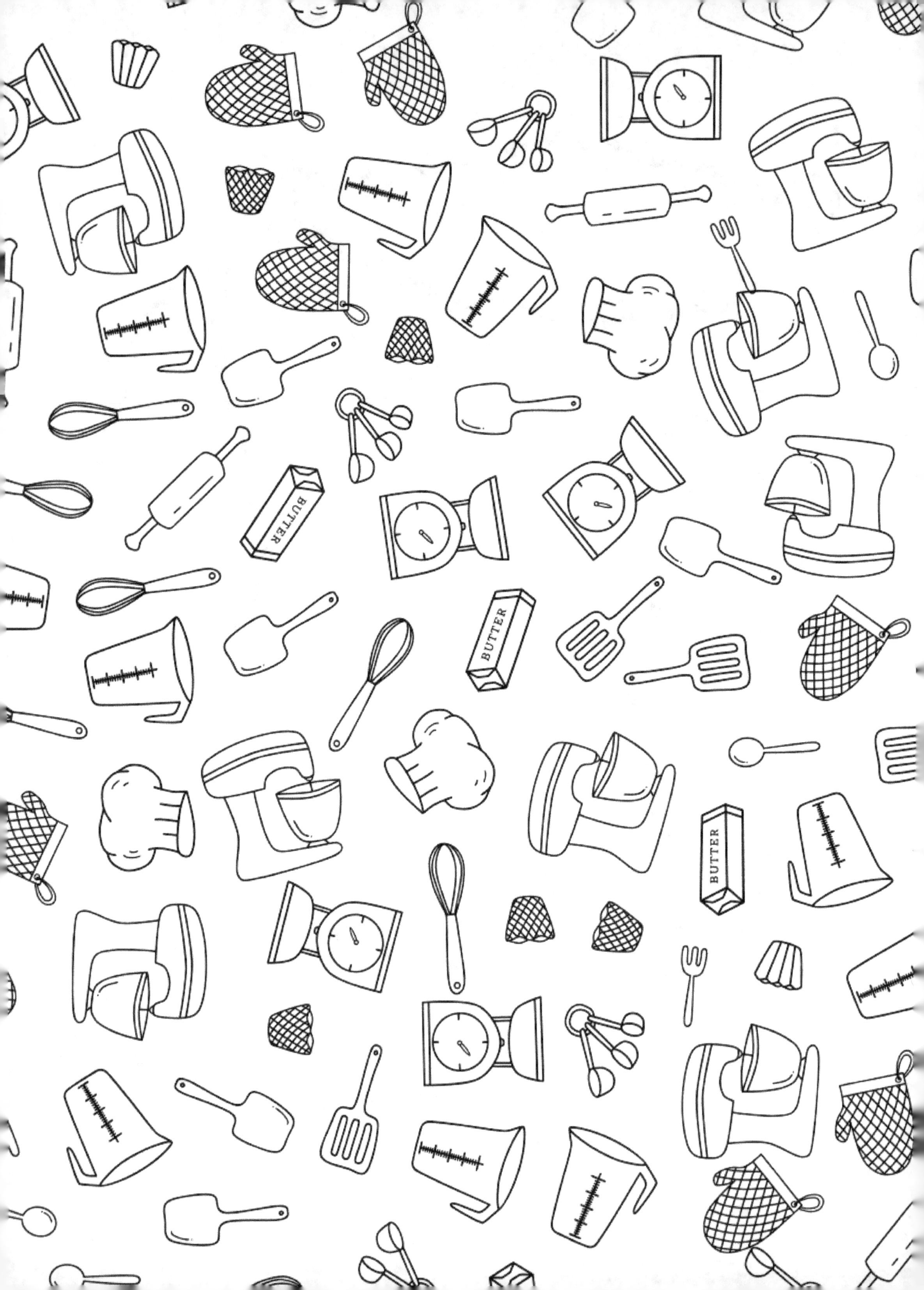

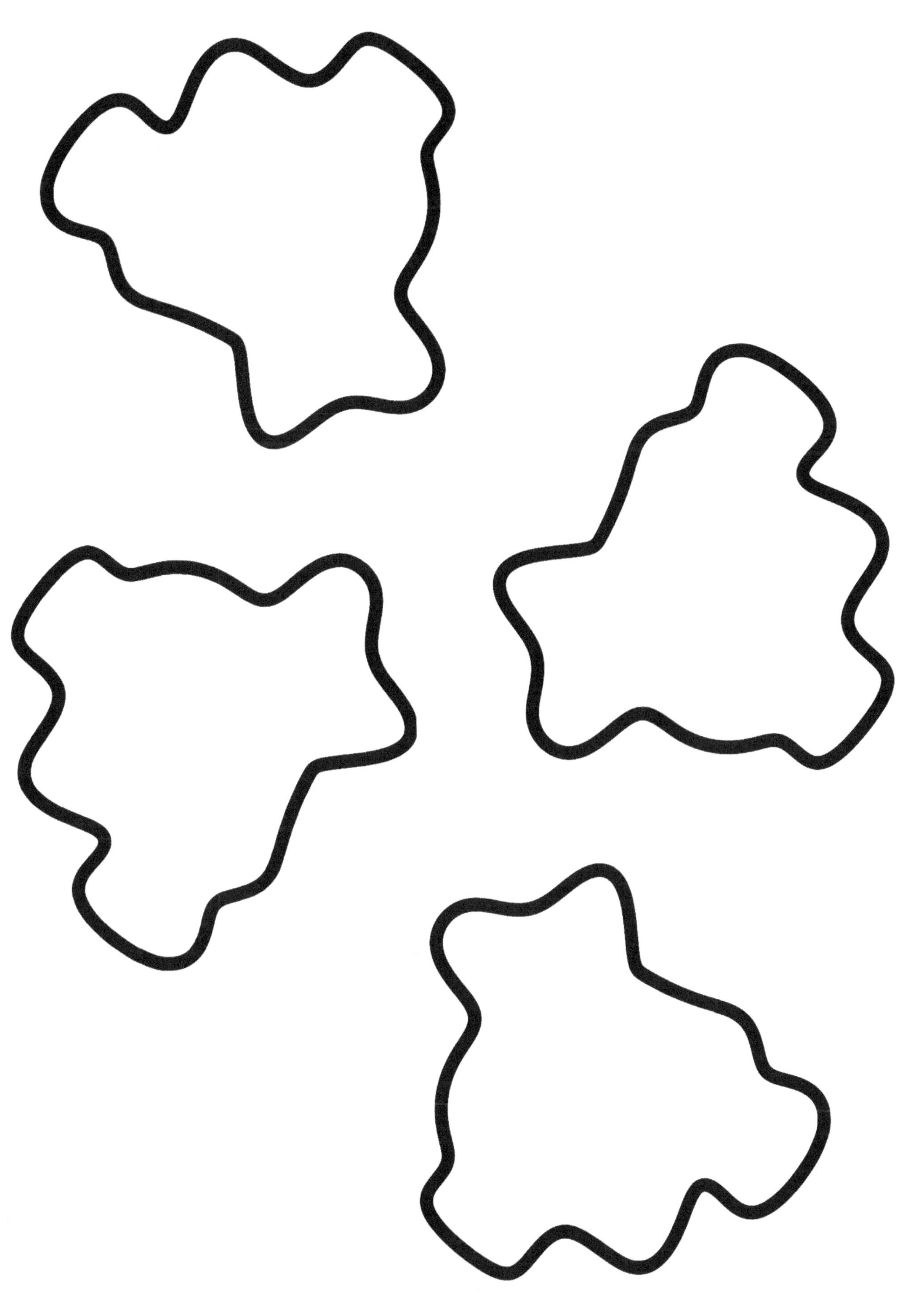

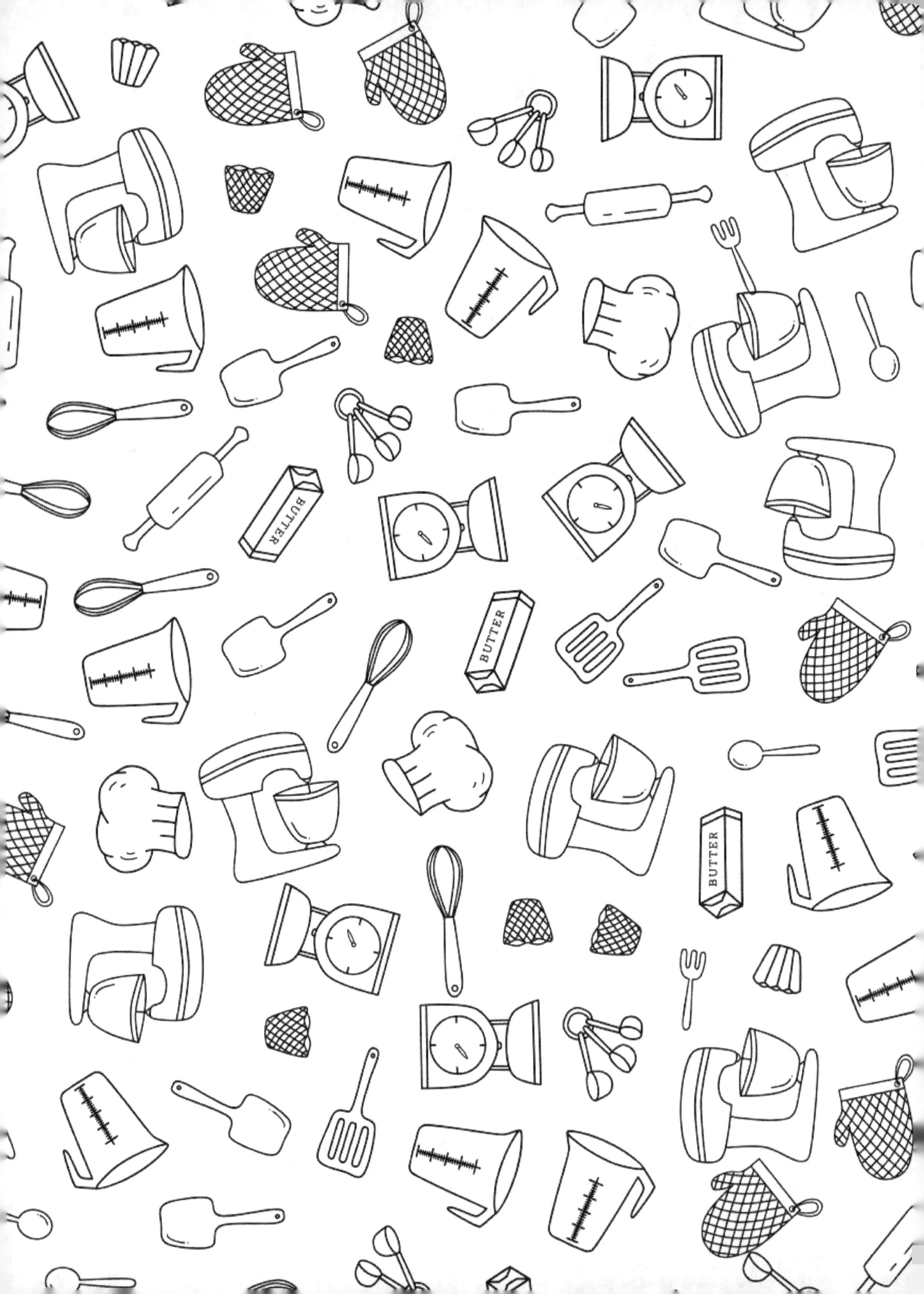

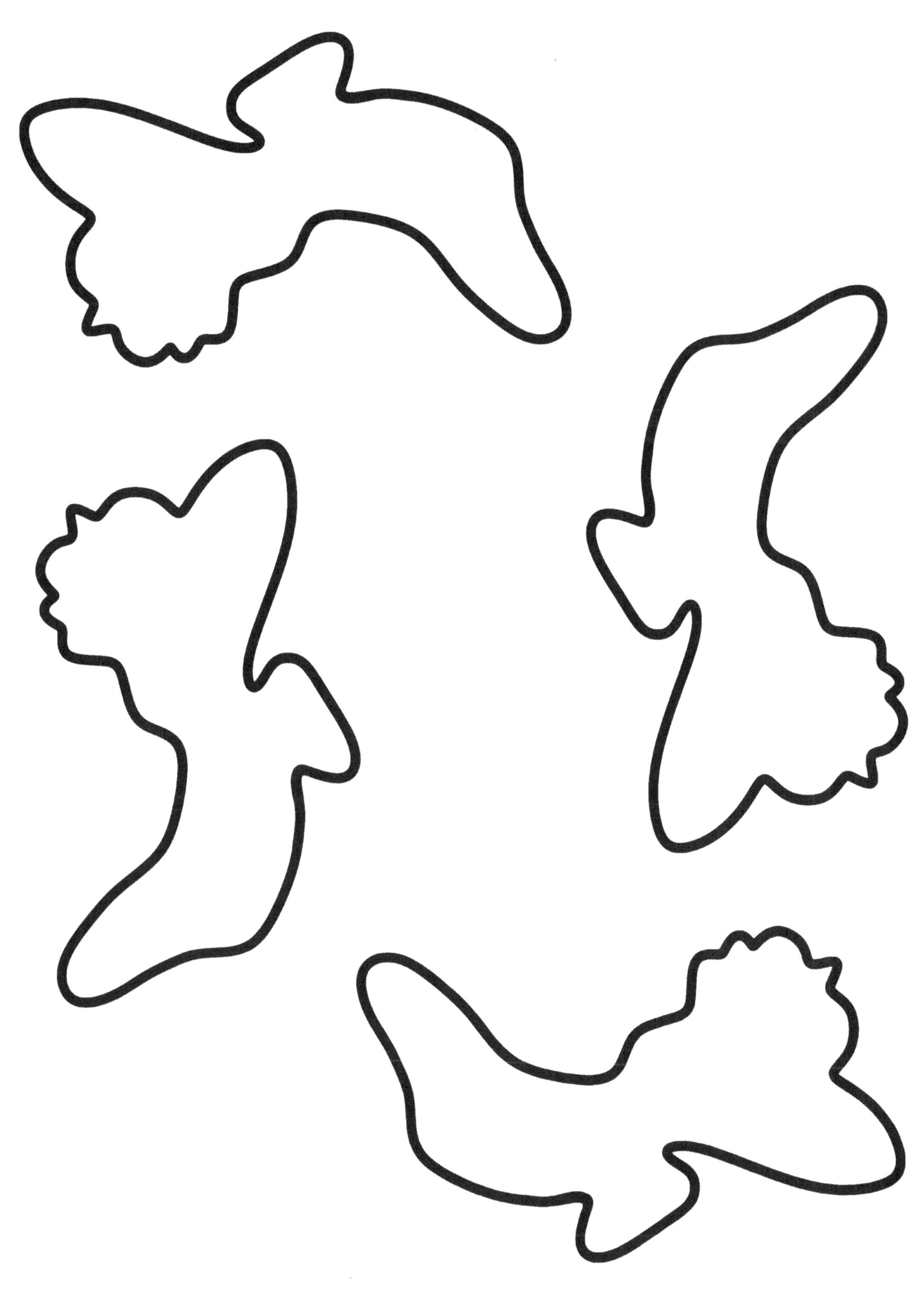

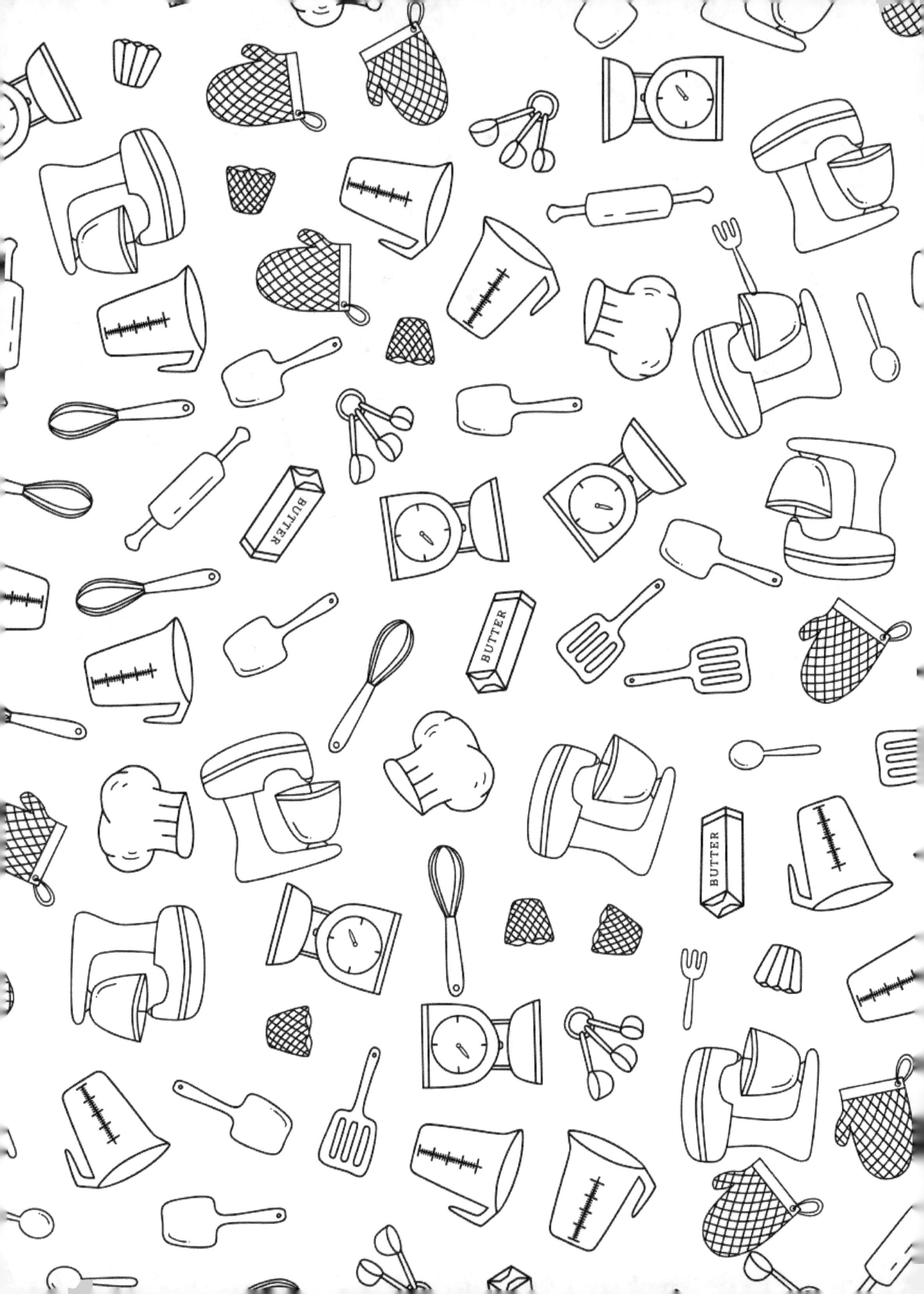

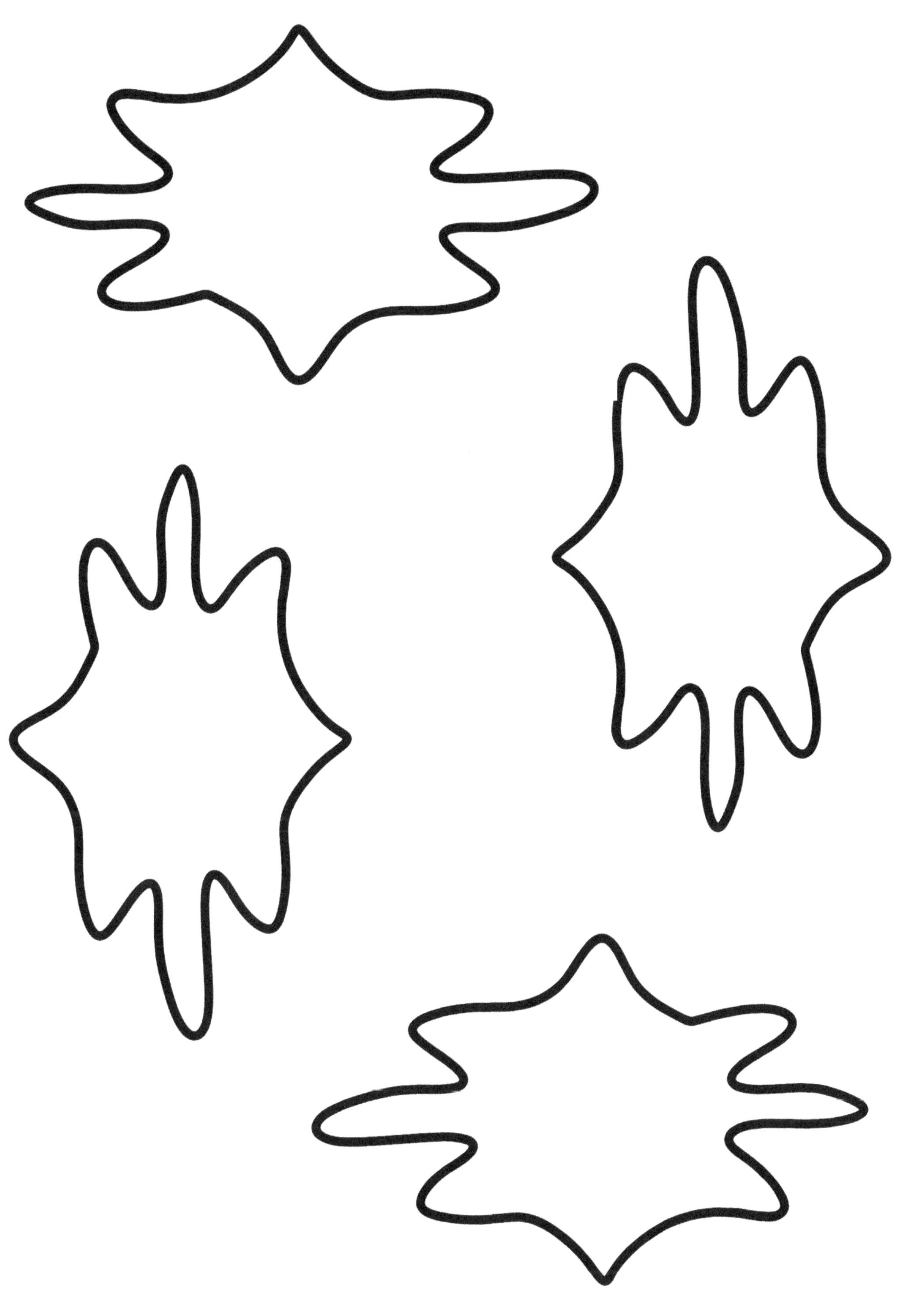

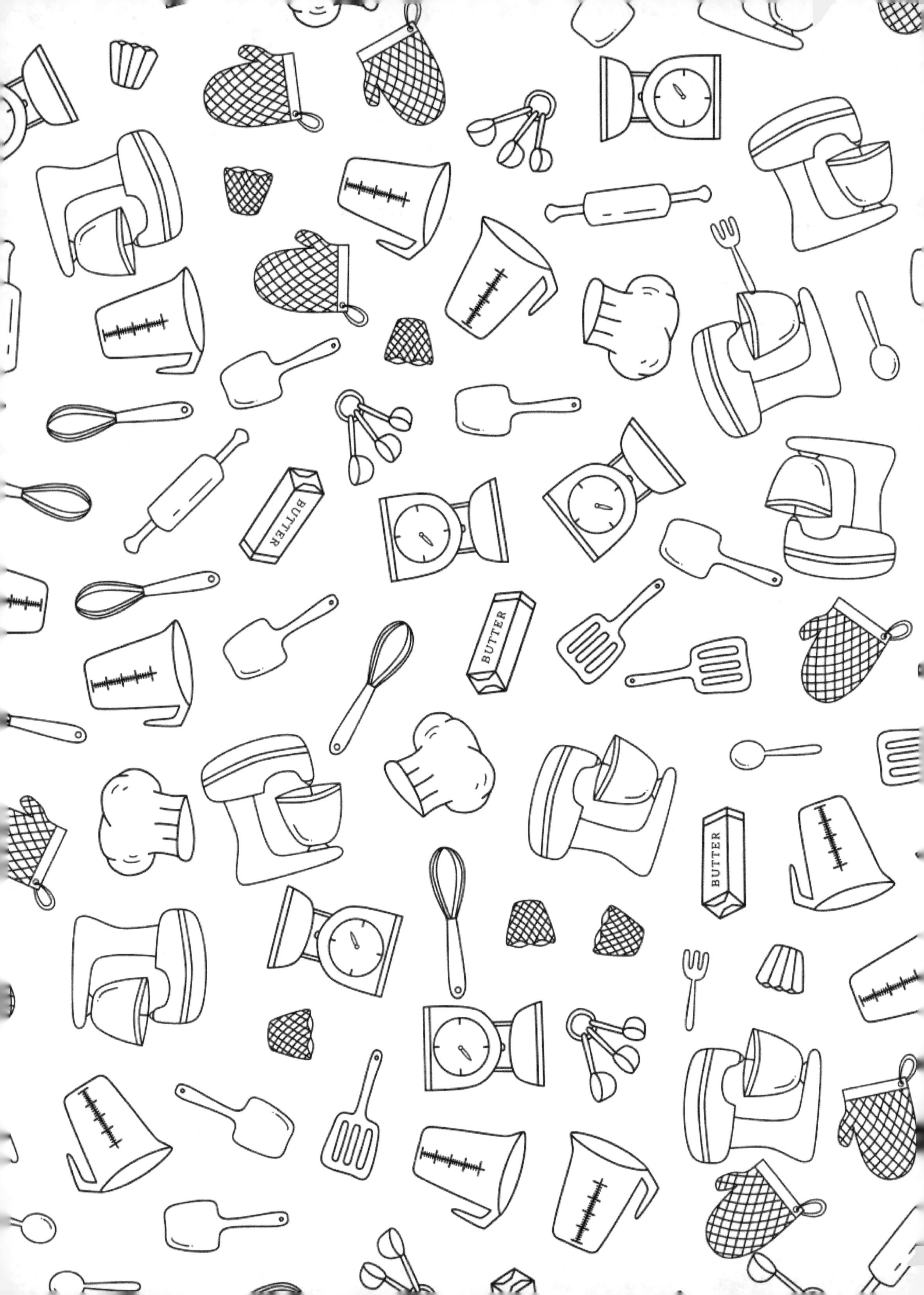

BUTTER
BUTTER
BUTTER

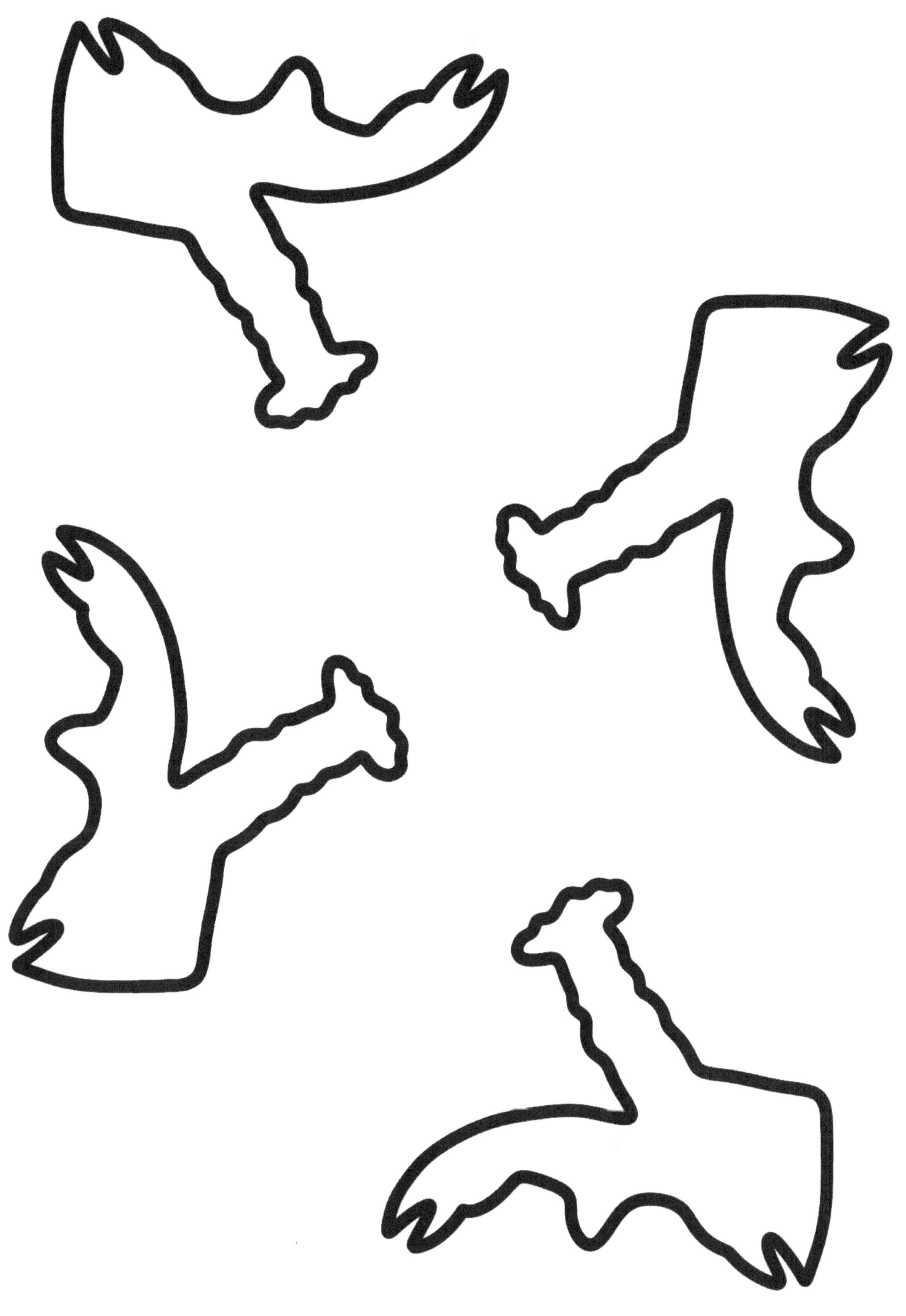

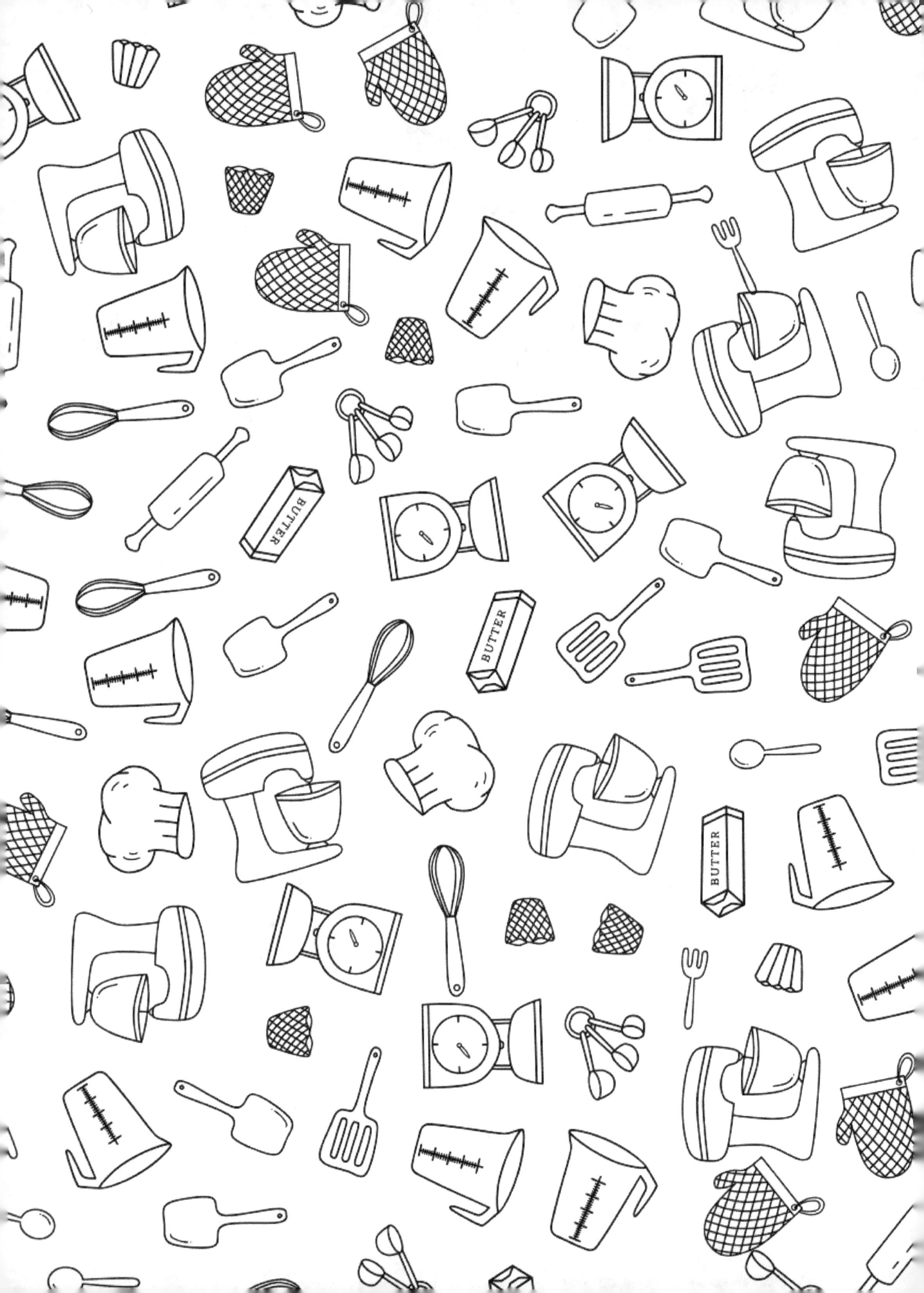

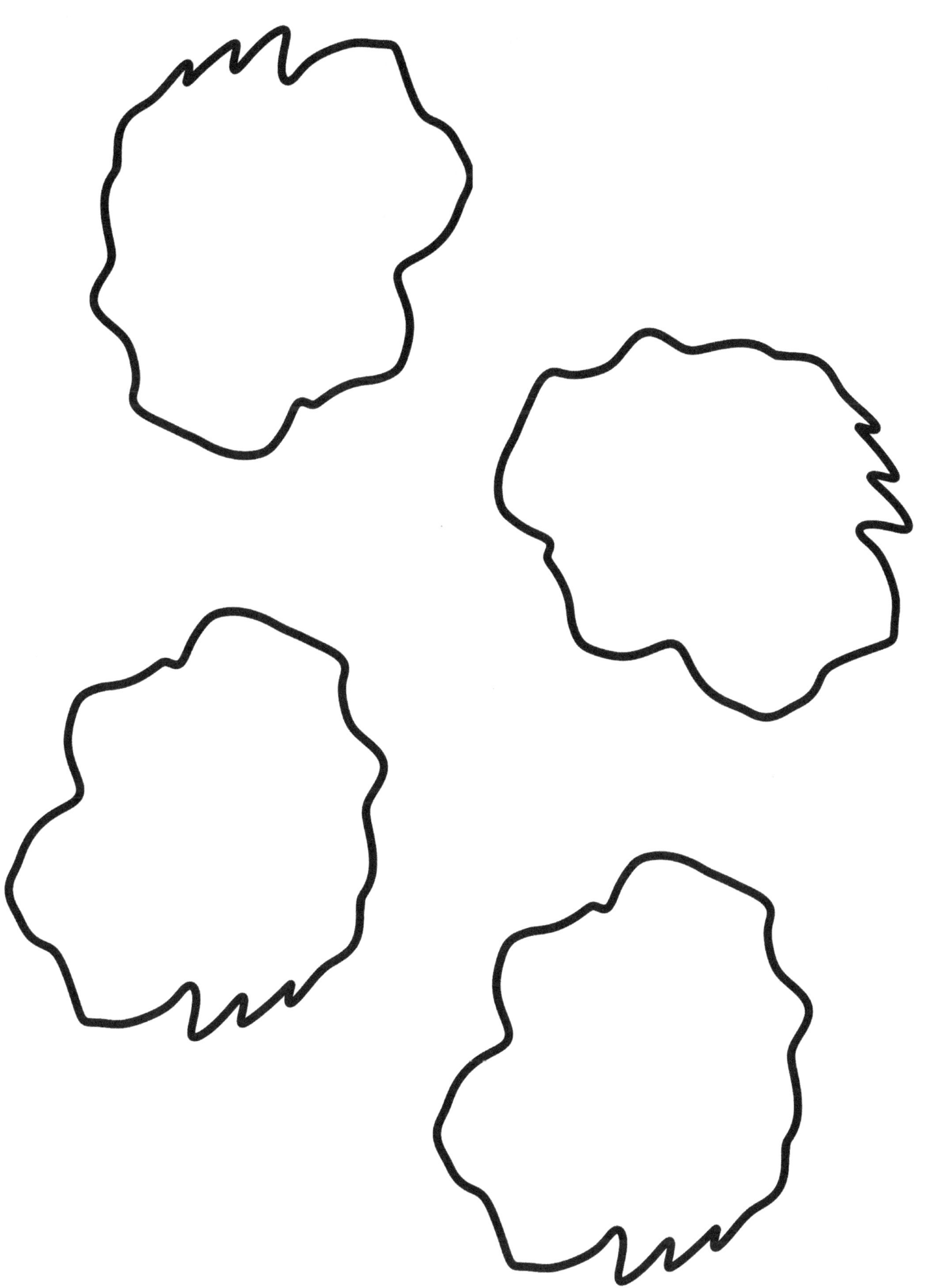

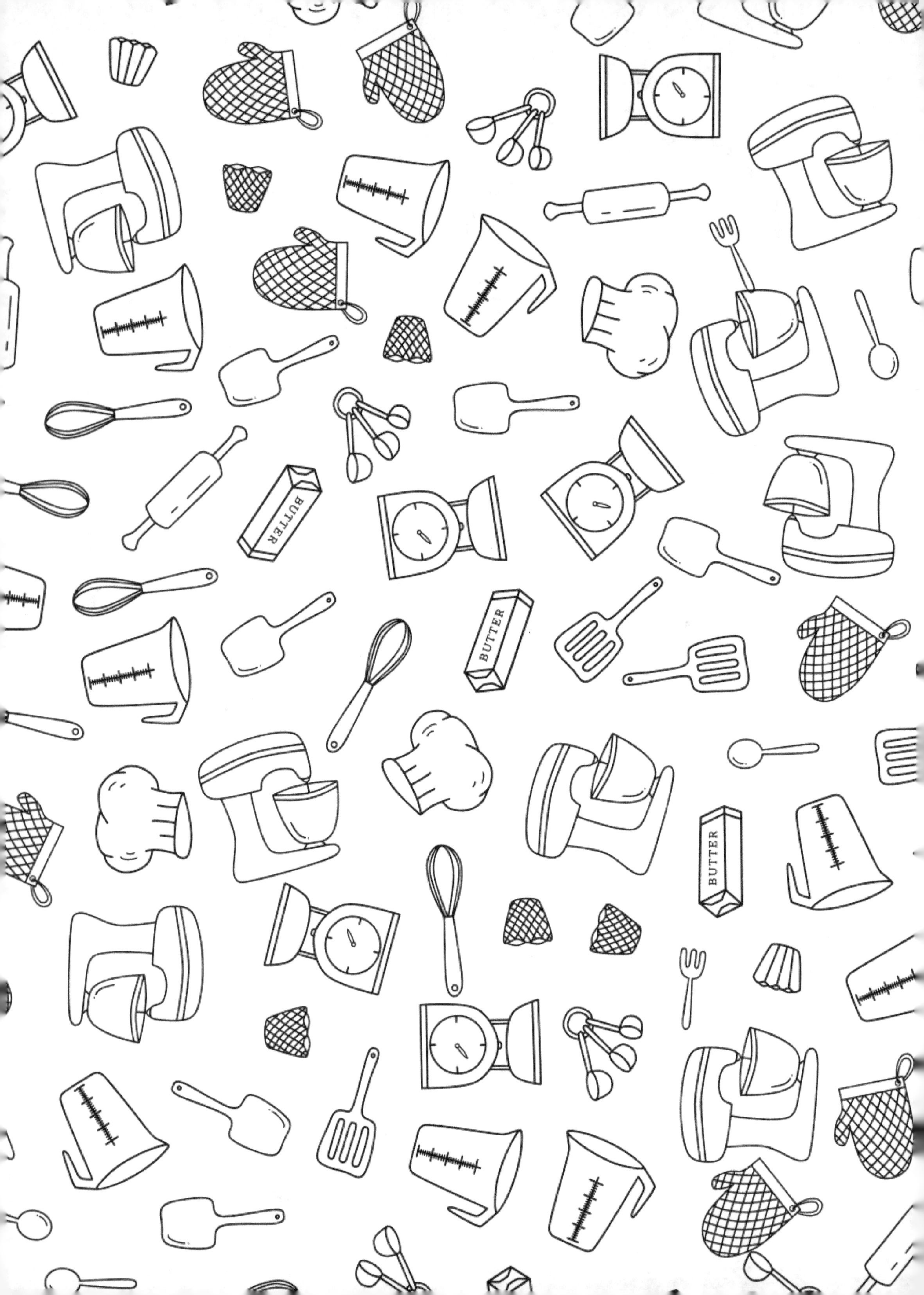

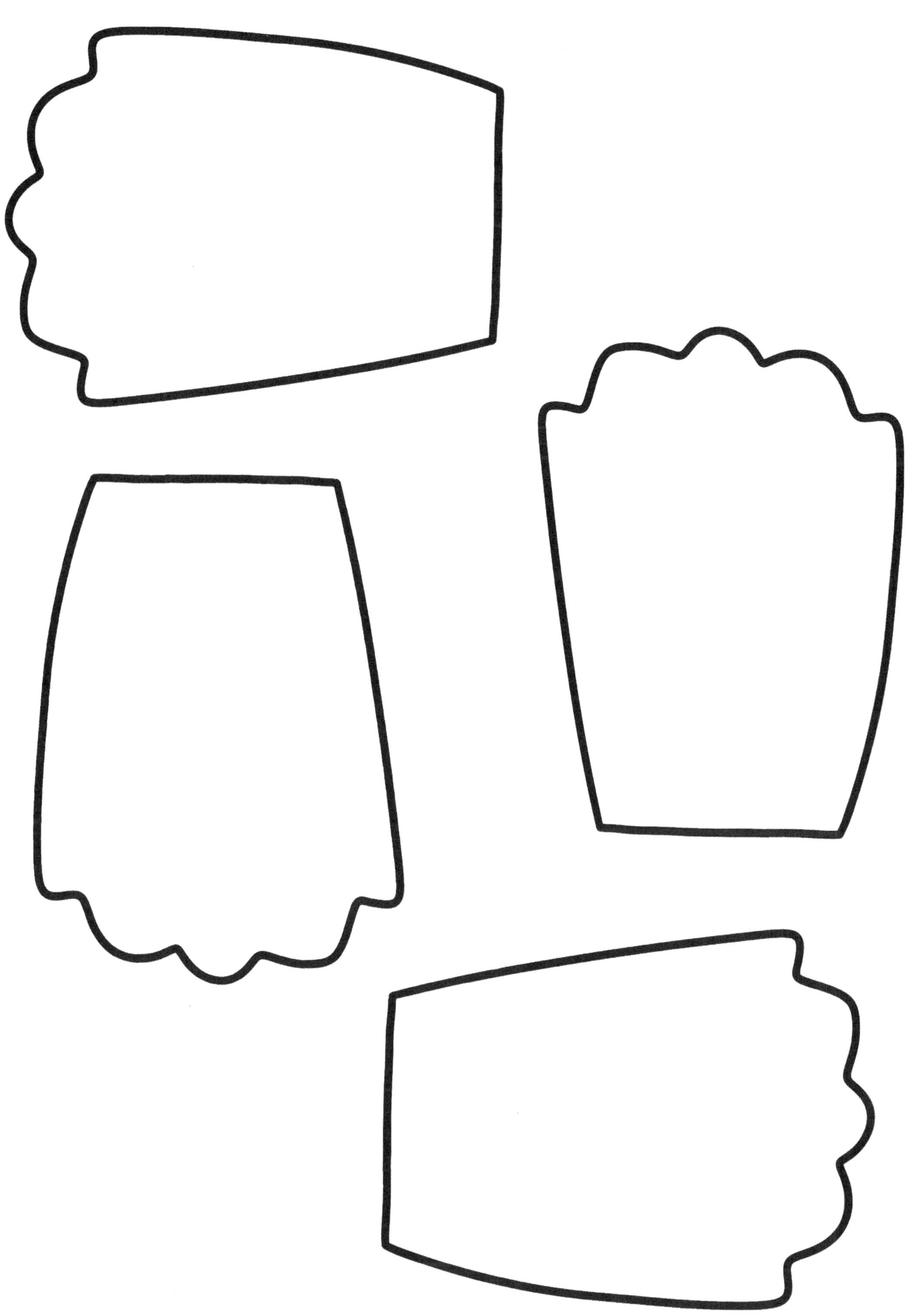

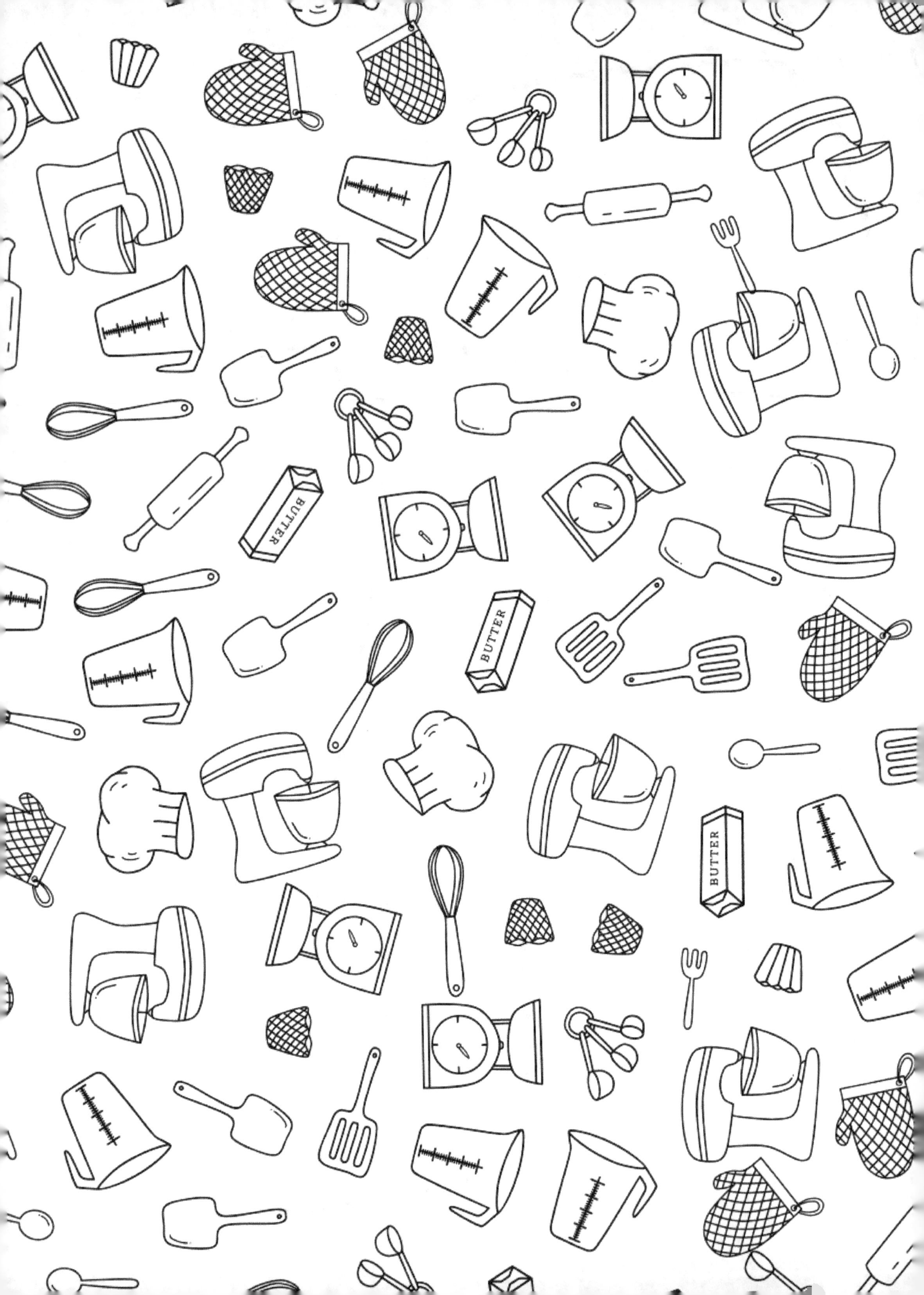

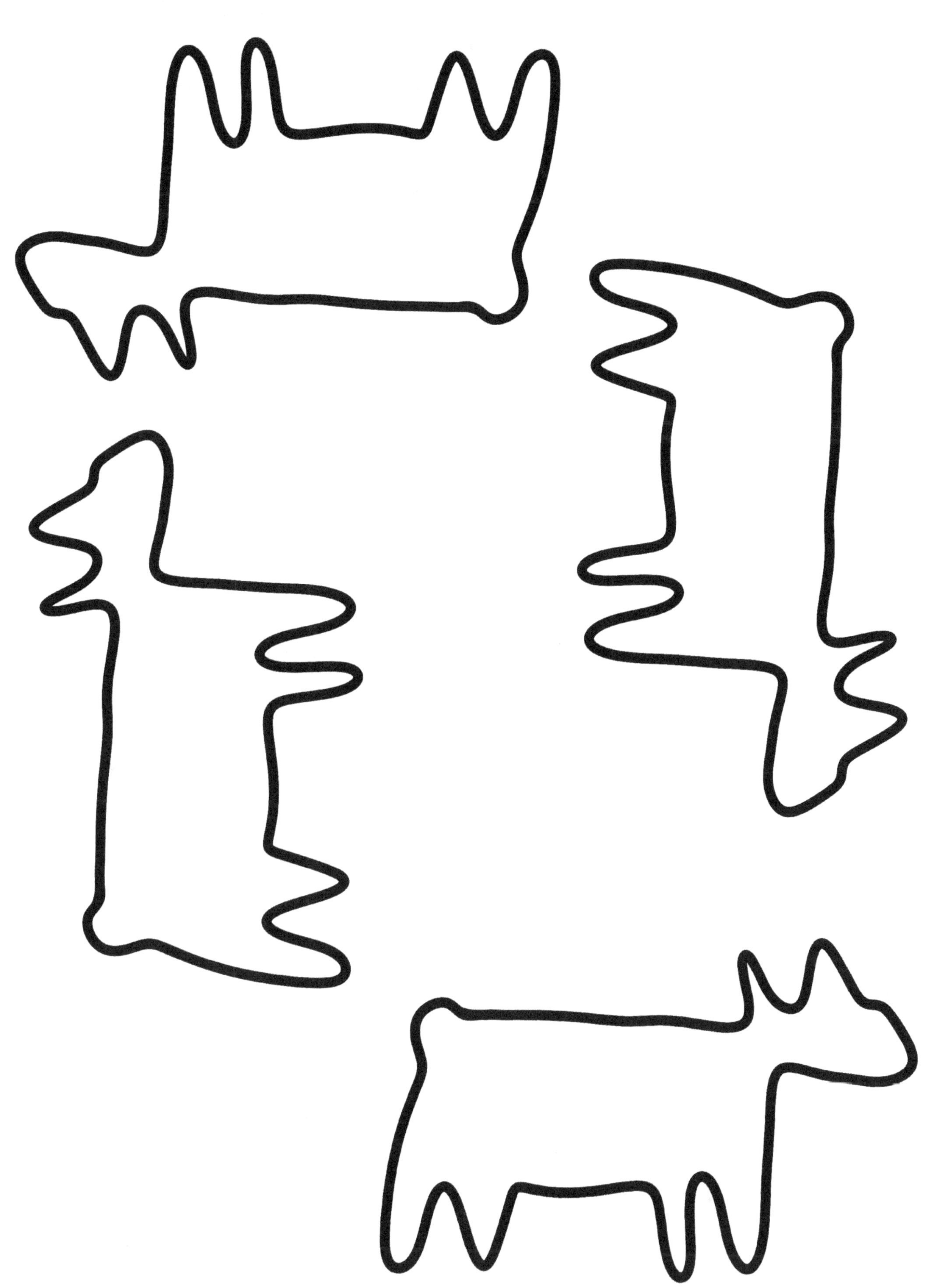

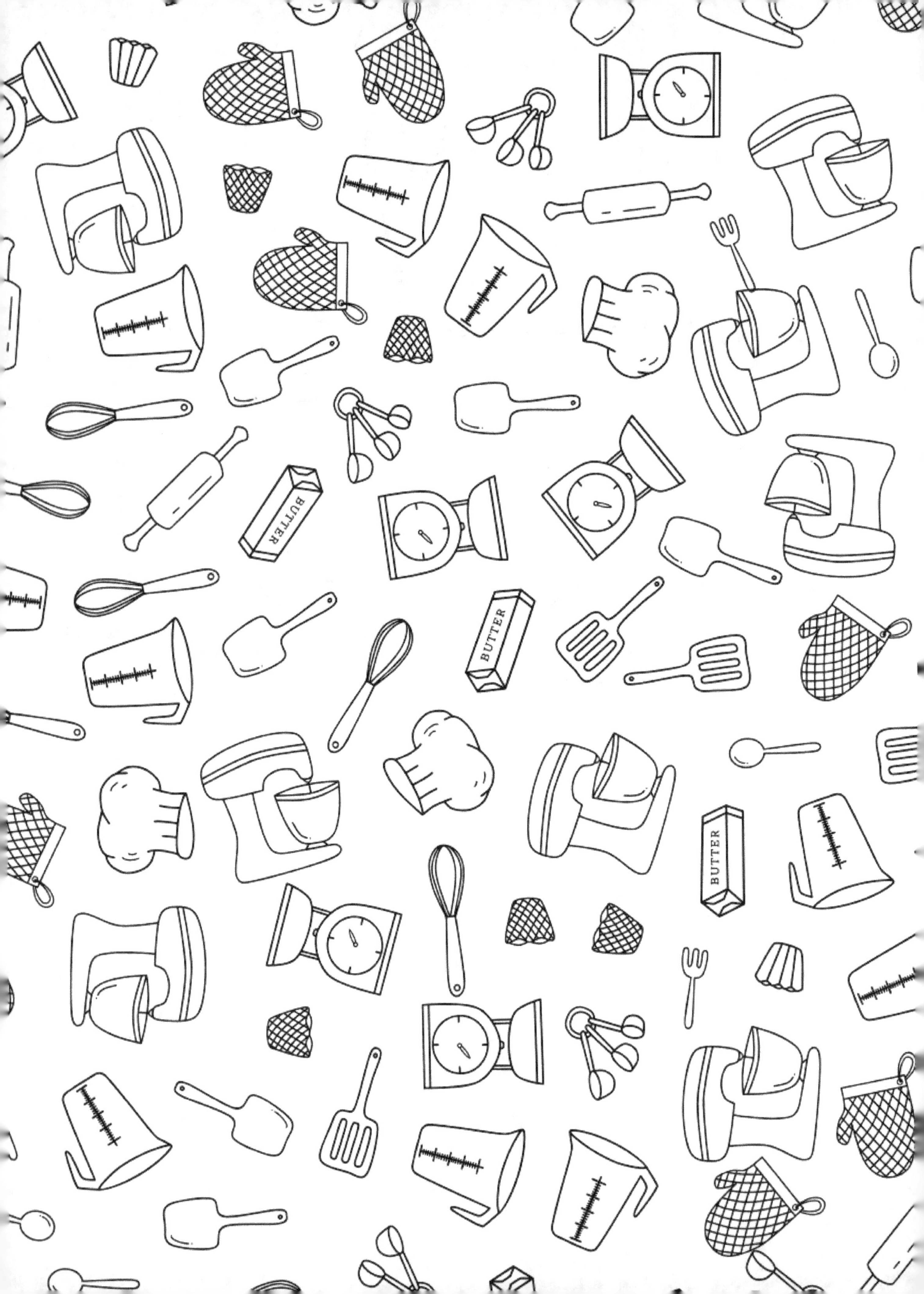
BUTTER
BUTTER
BUTTER

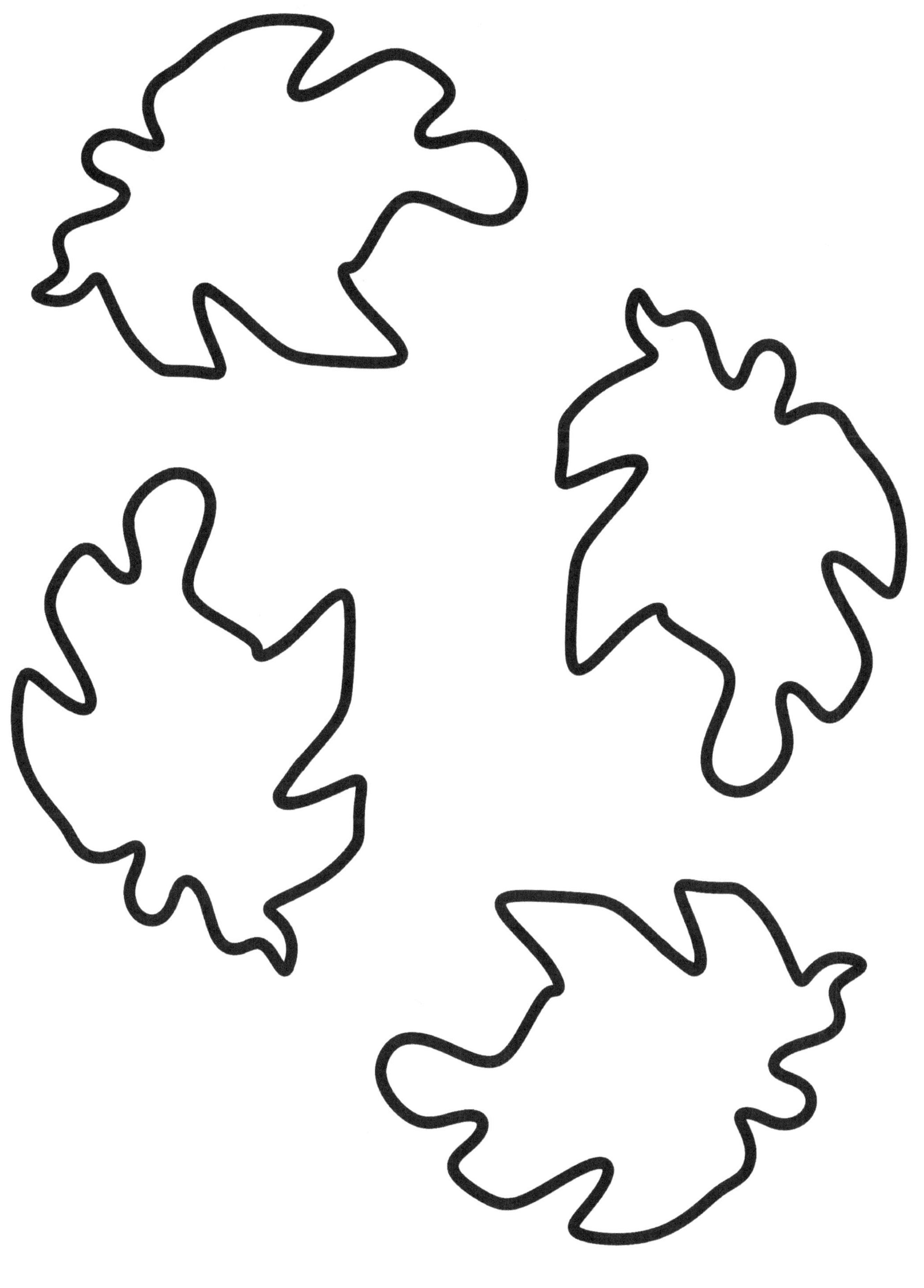

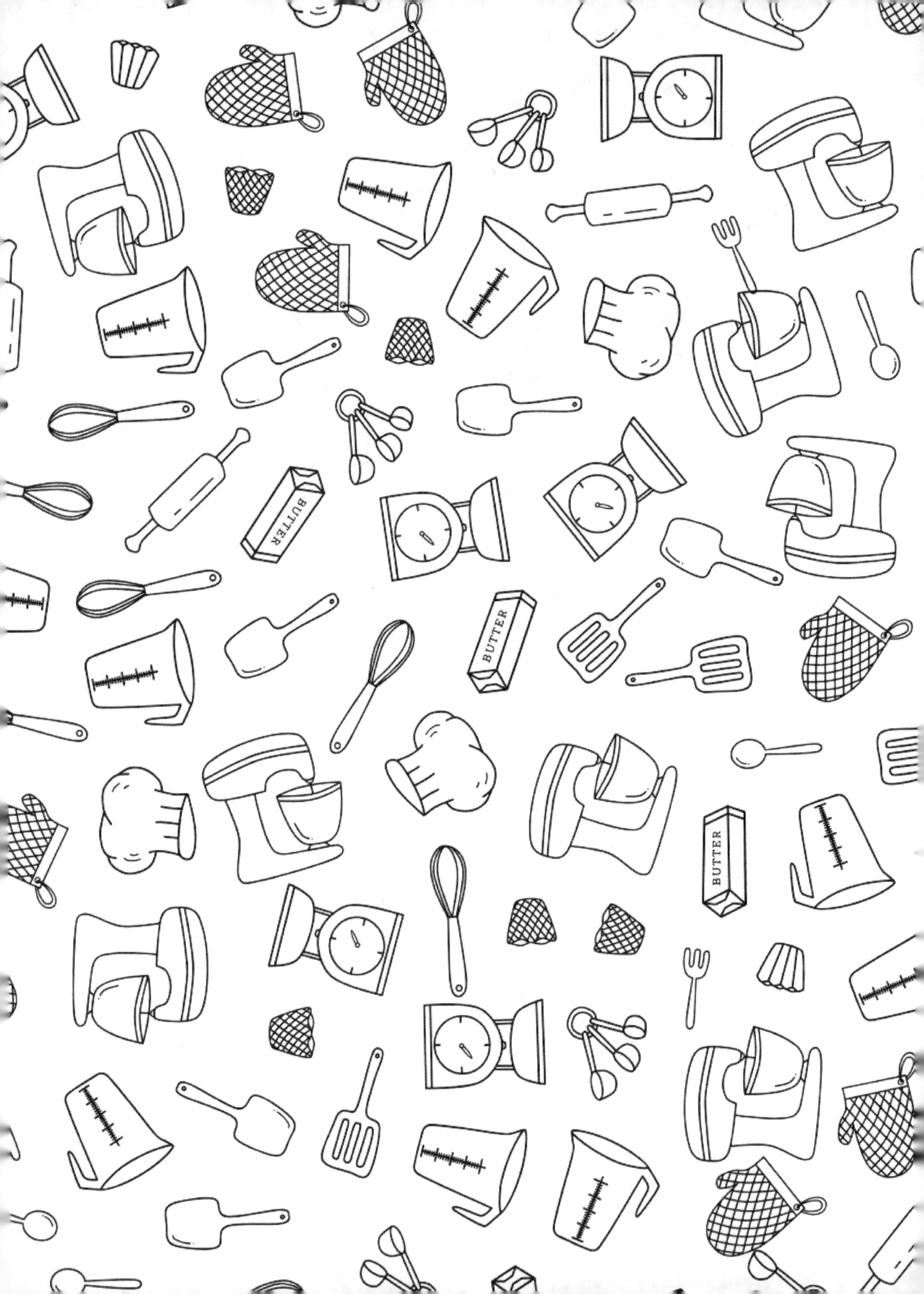

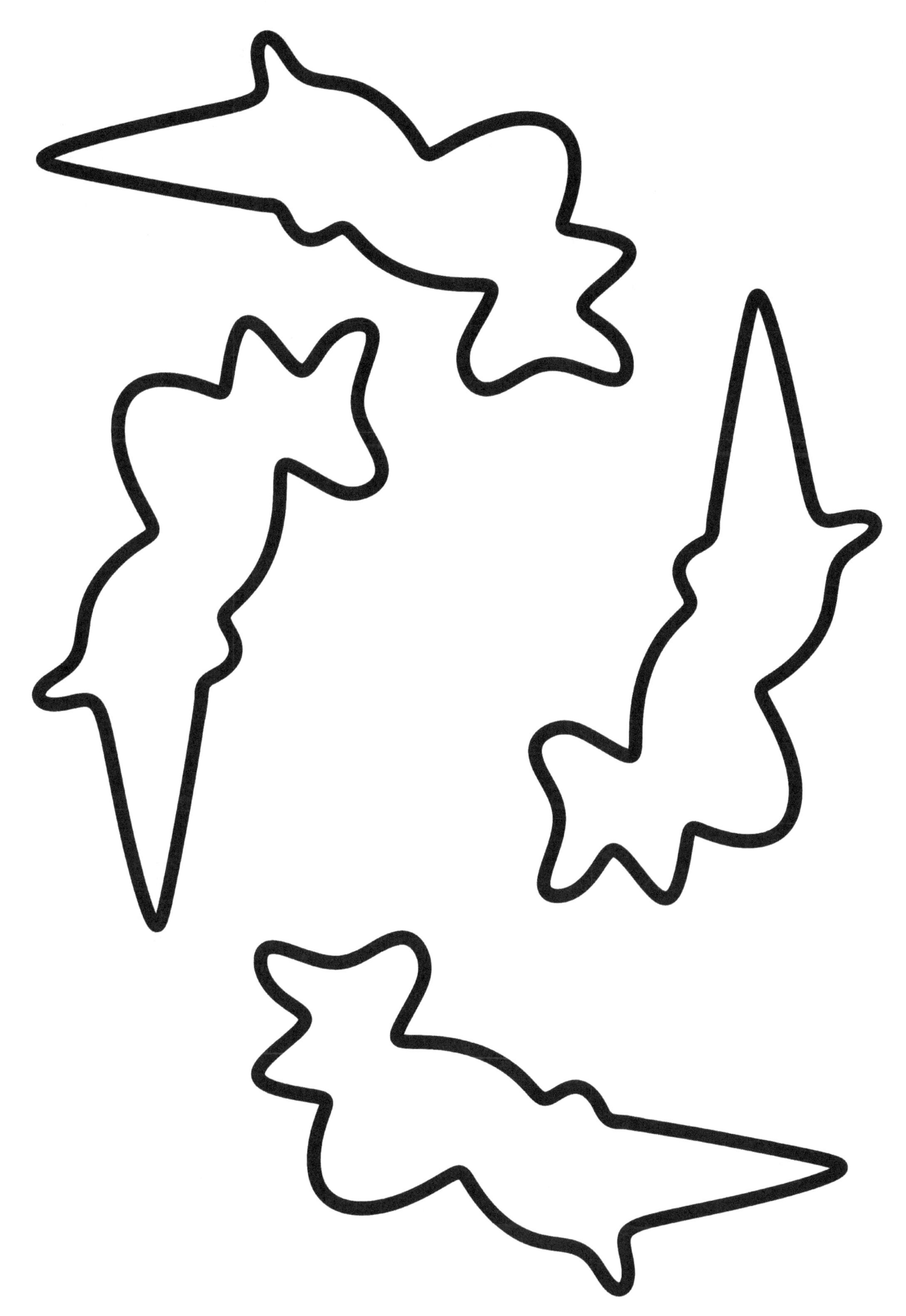

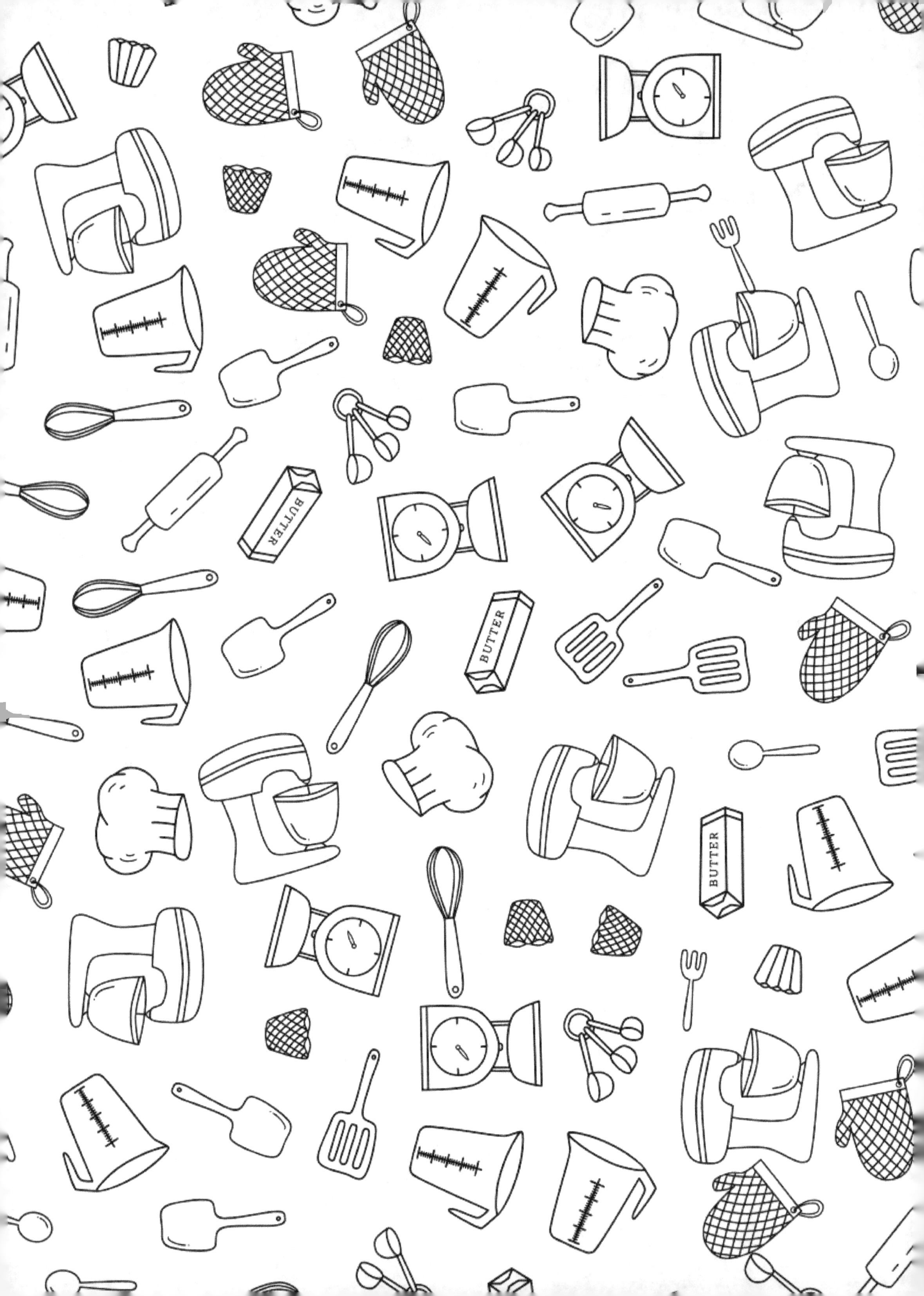

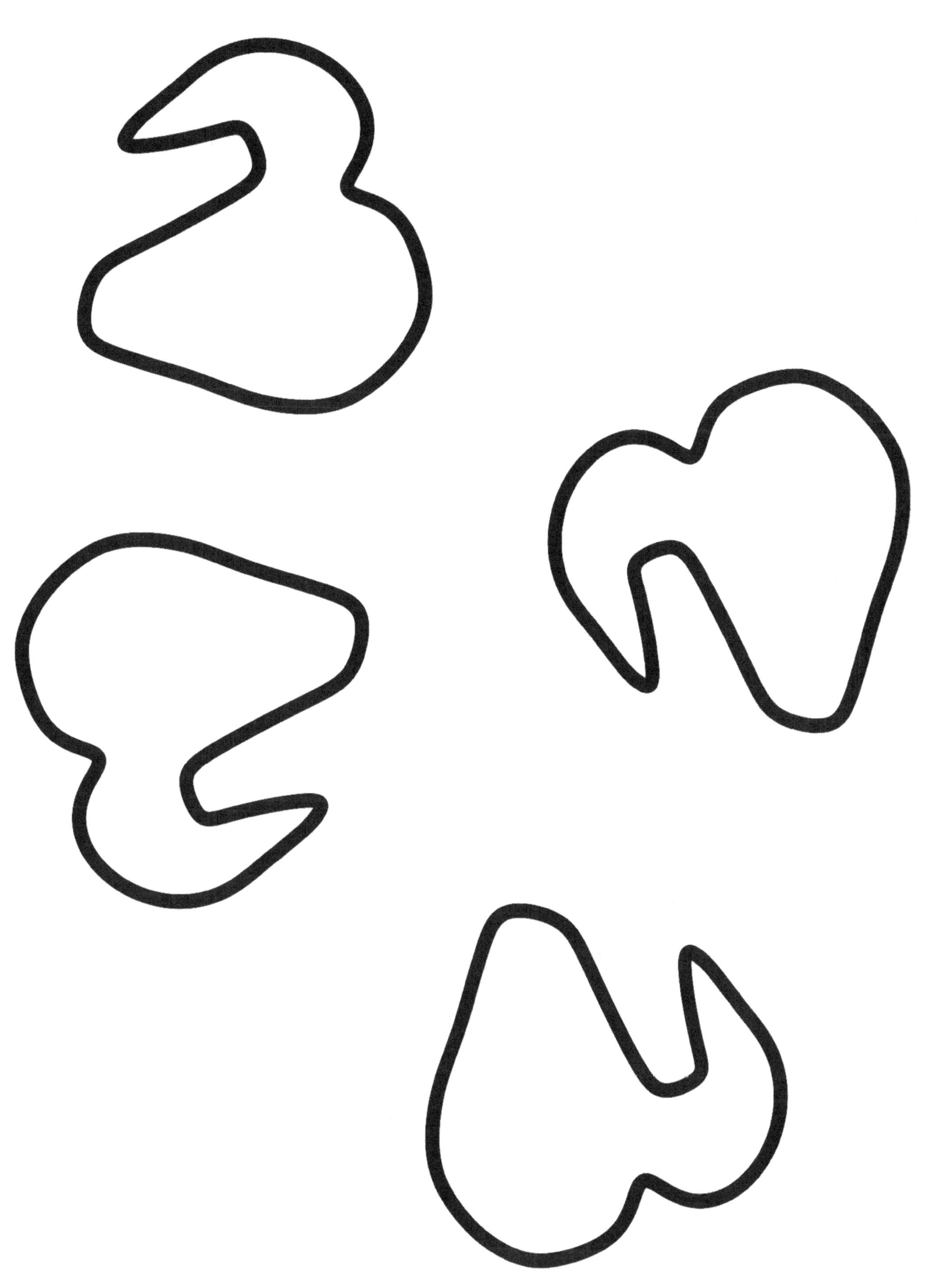

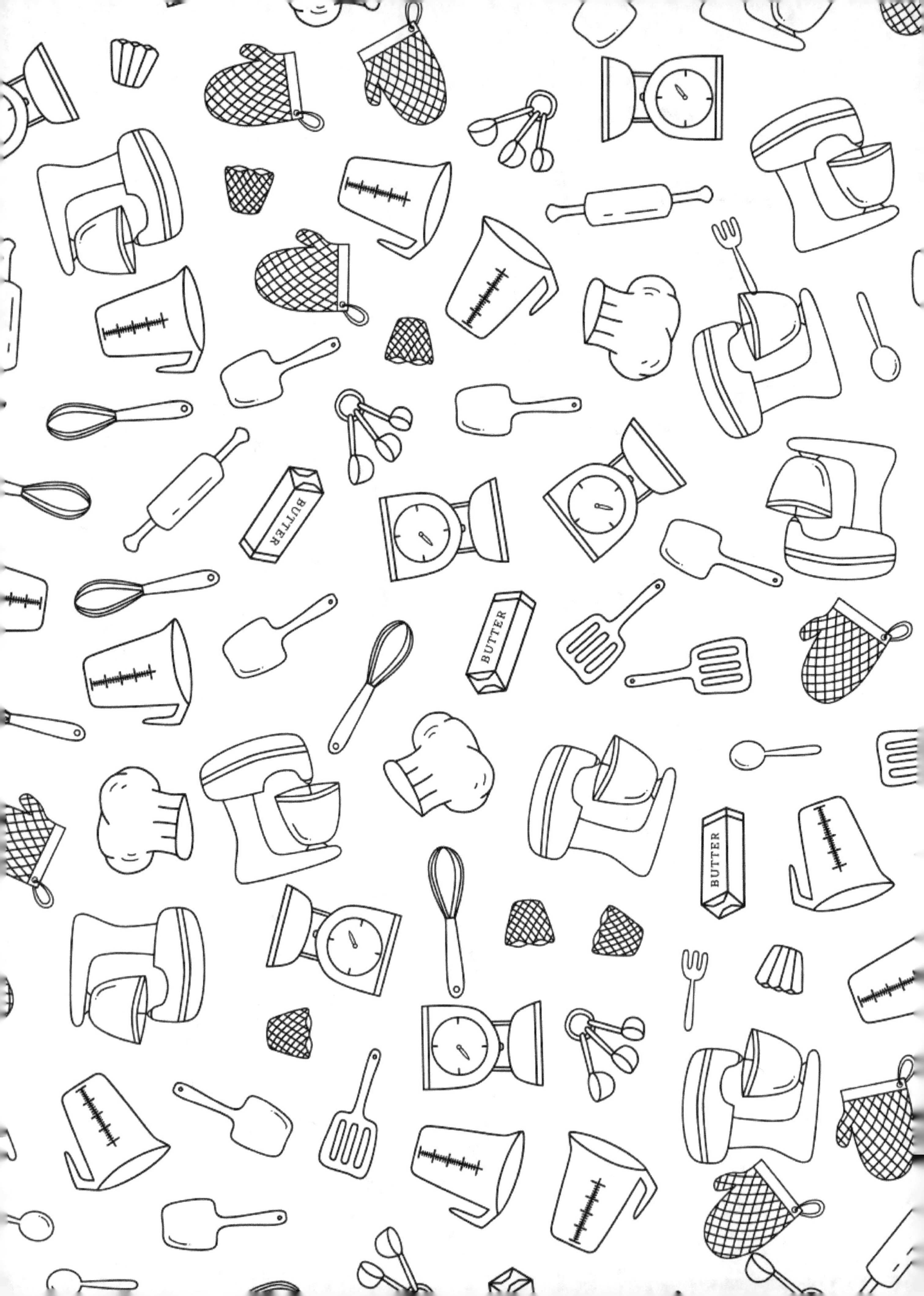
BUTTER
BUTTER
BUTTER

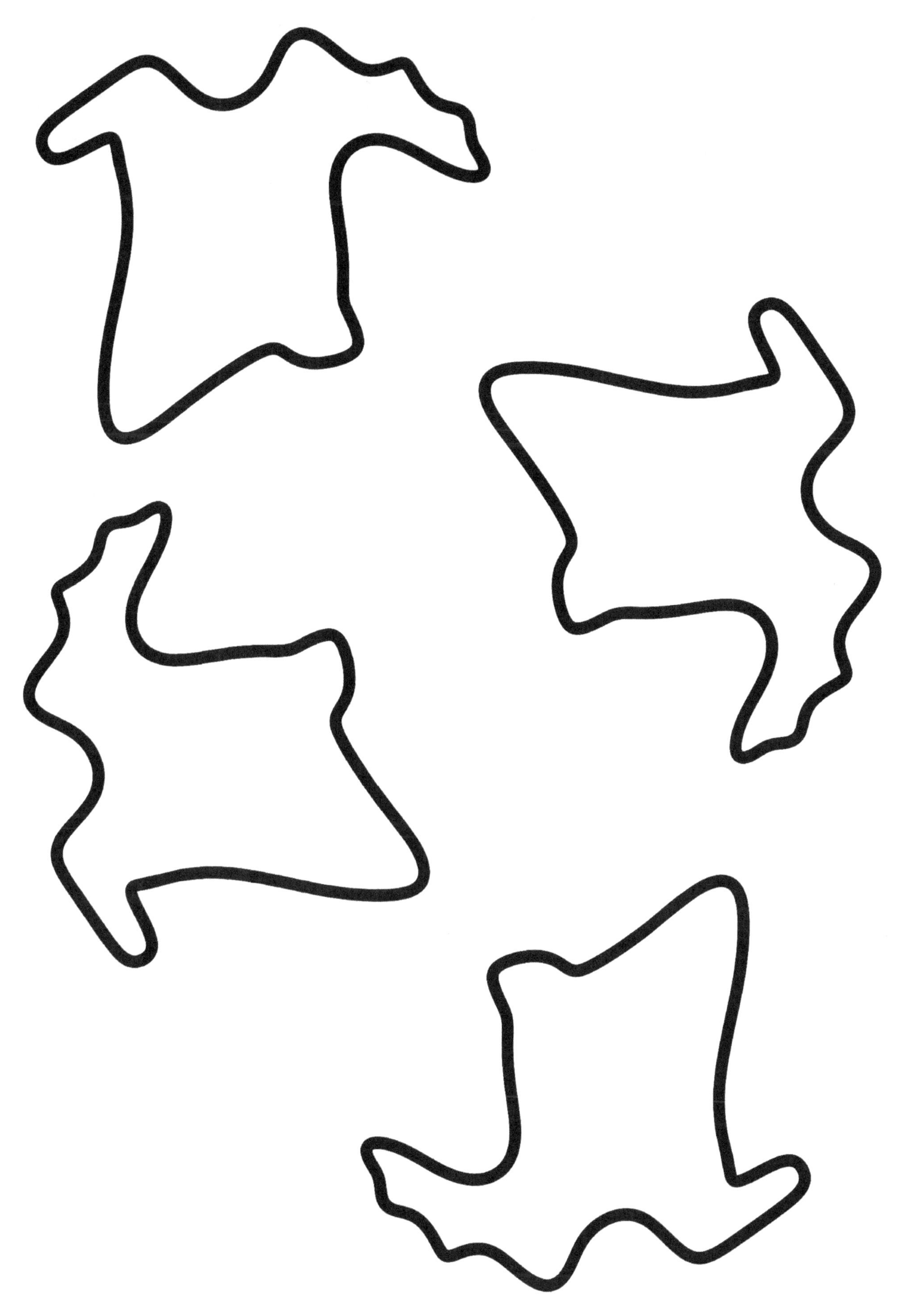

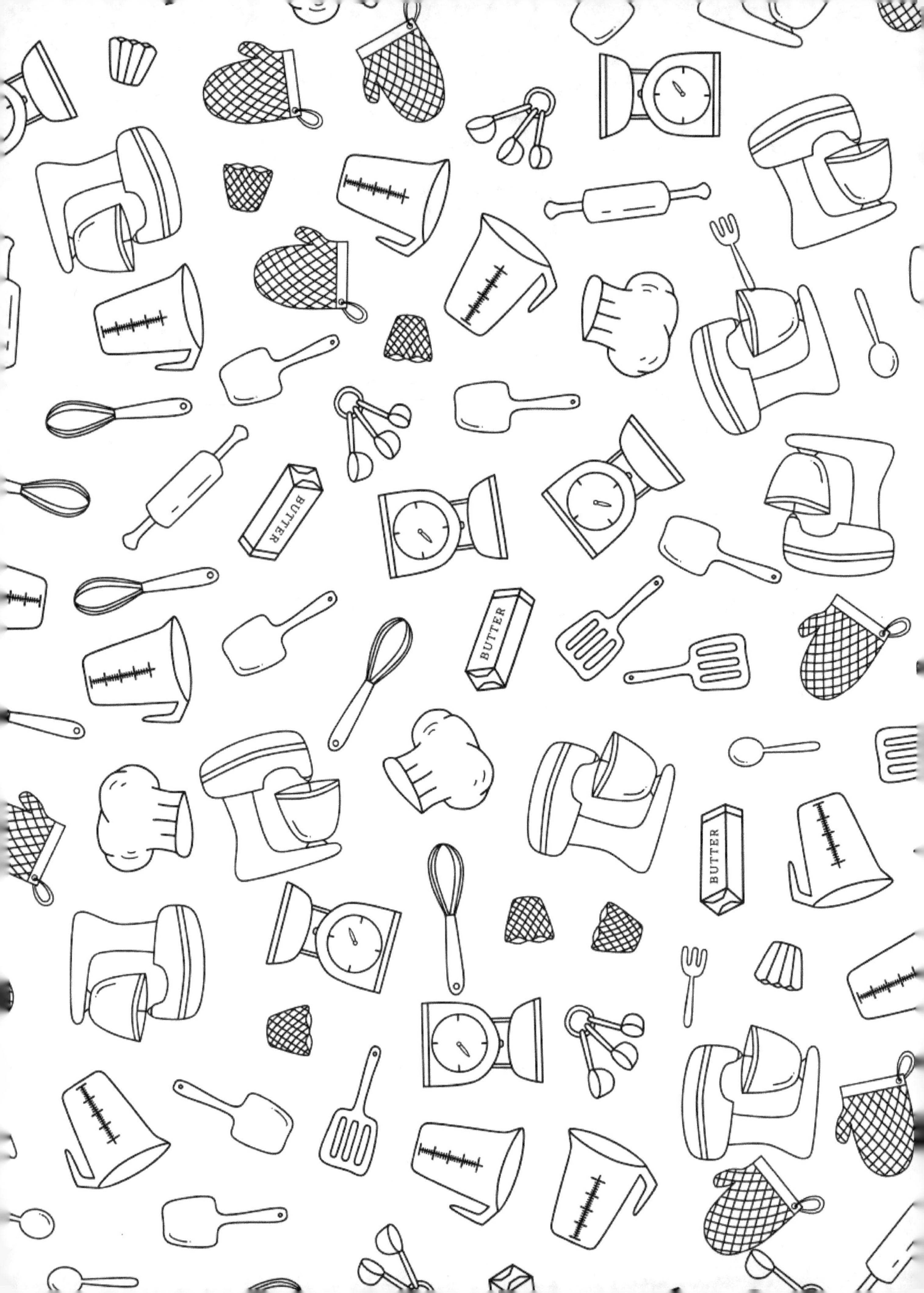

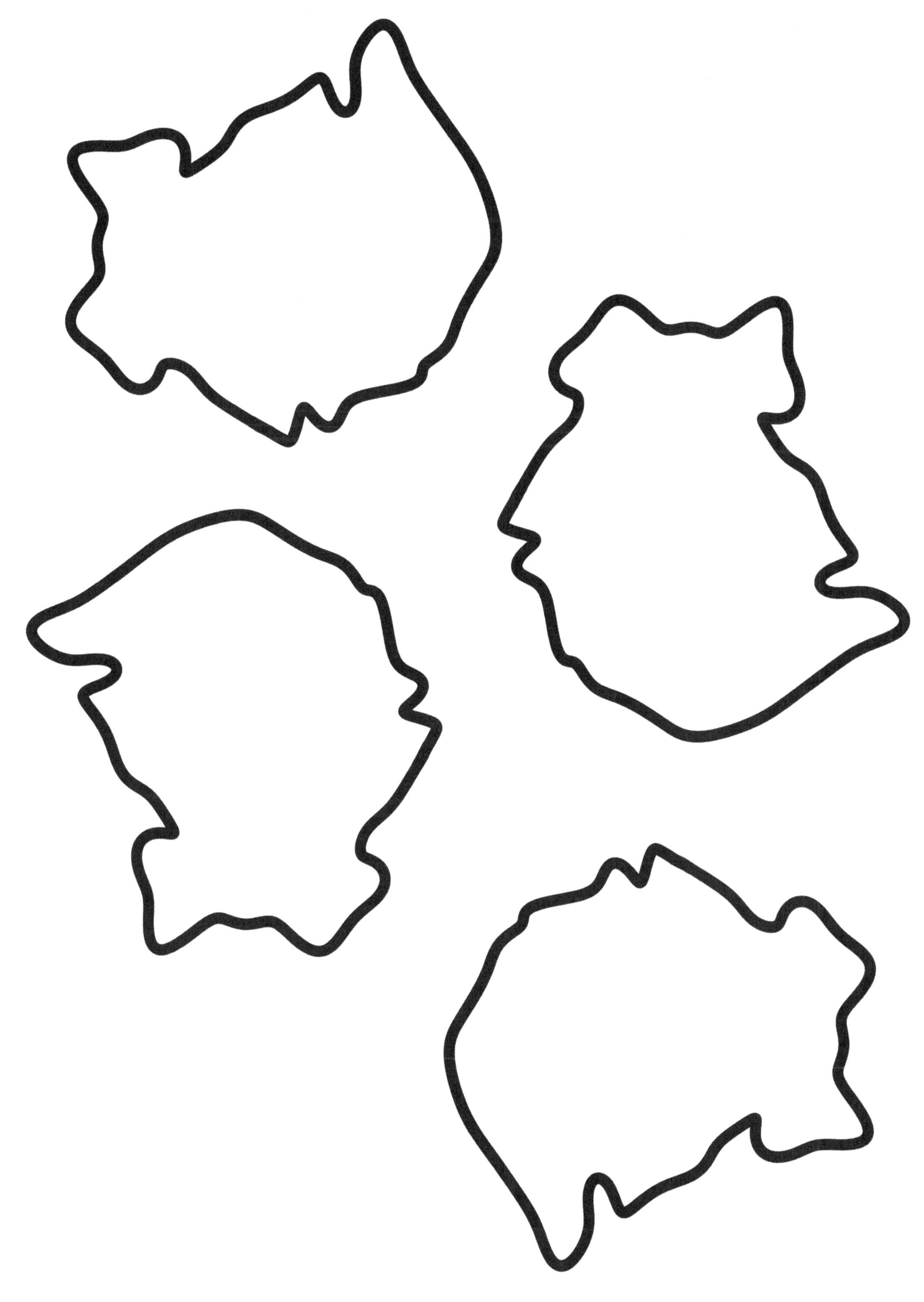

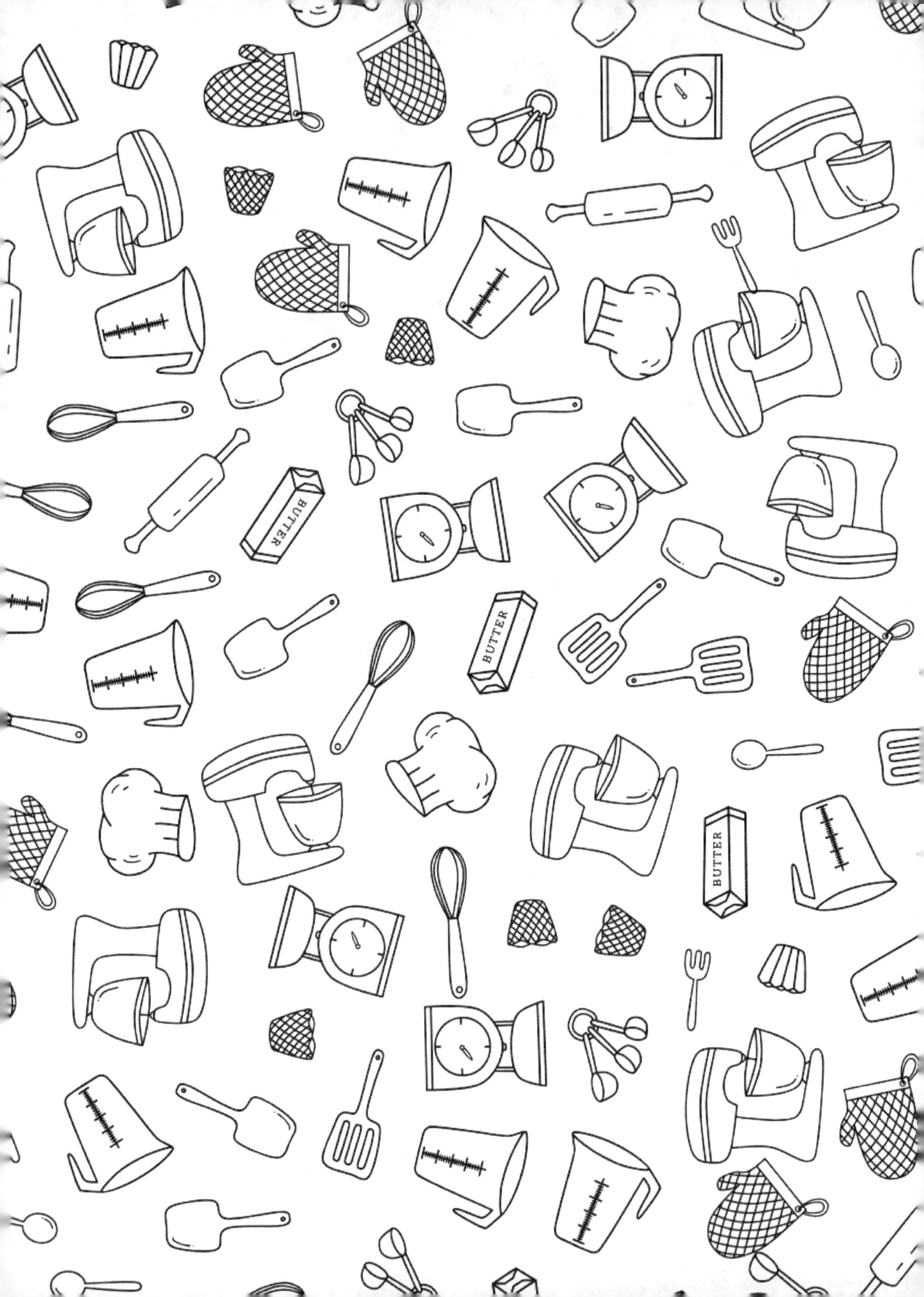

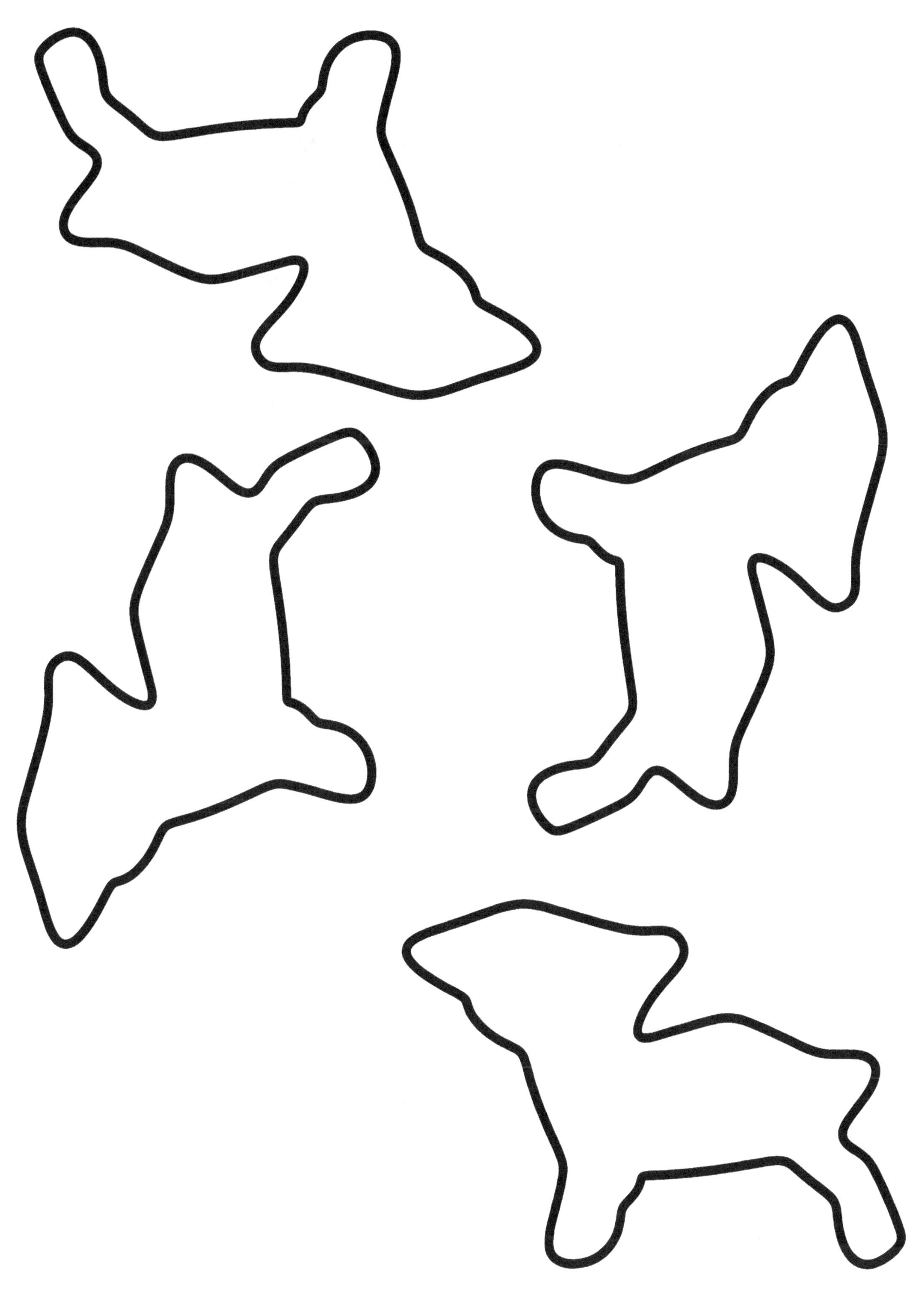

More Cookie Cutters Coming Soon!

Until Then, Check Out Our Other Amazing Books!

www.likespublishing.com

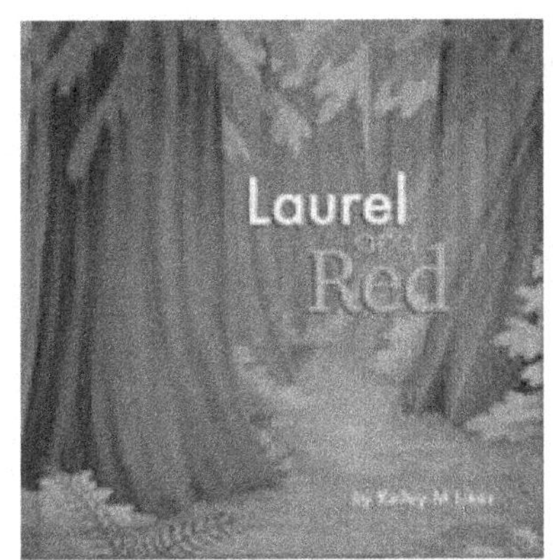
Laurel
and
Red
by Kelley M Likes

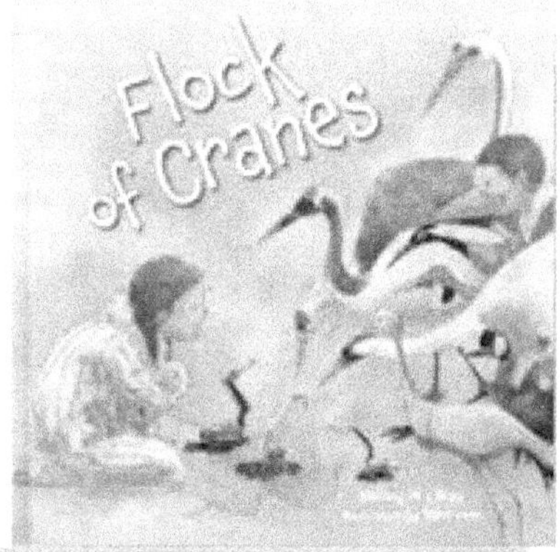
Flock
of Cranes

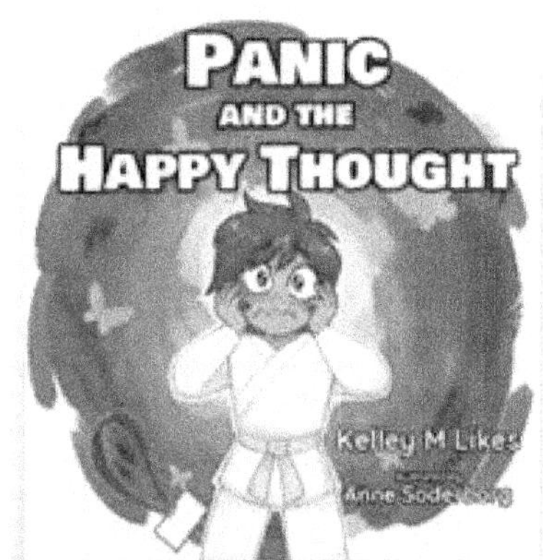
PANIC
AND THE
HAPPY THOUGHT
Kelley M Likes
Anne Soderborg

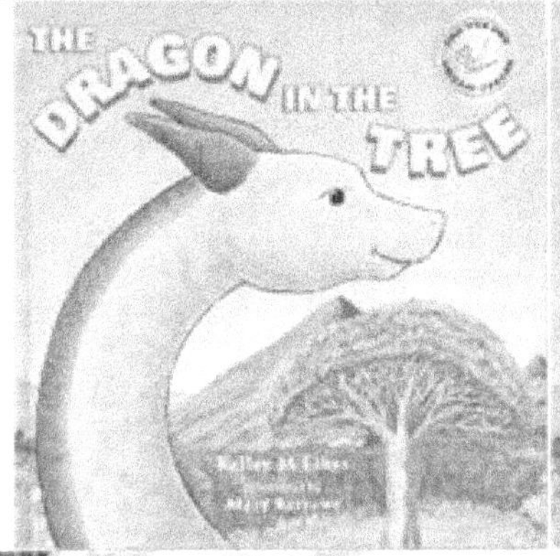
THE
DRAGON IN THE TREE
Kelley M Likes
Mary Barrows

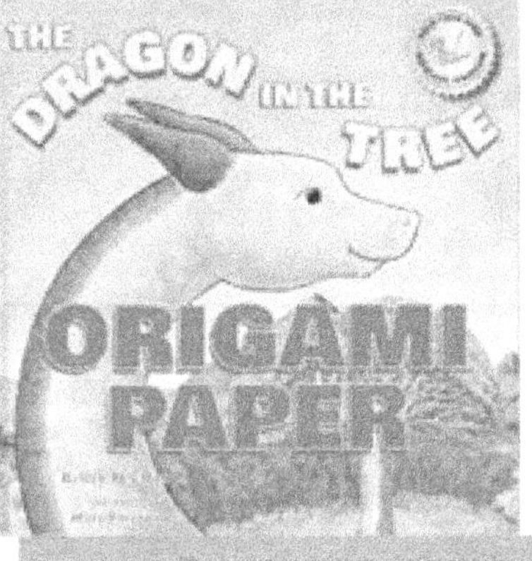
THE
DRAGON IN THE TREE
ORIGAMI
PAPER

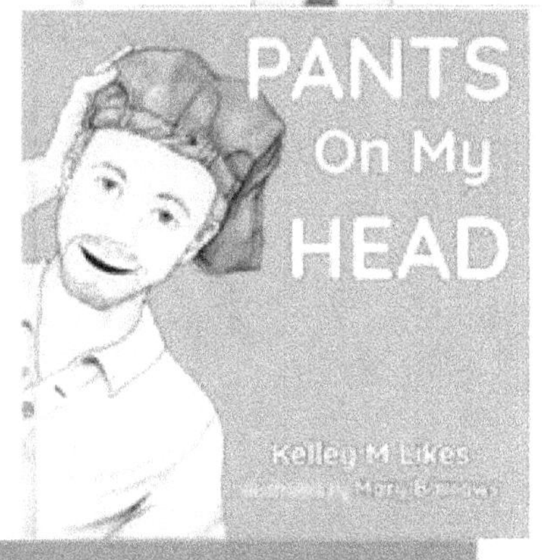
PANTS
On My
HEAD
Kelley M Likes
Mary Barrows

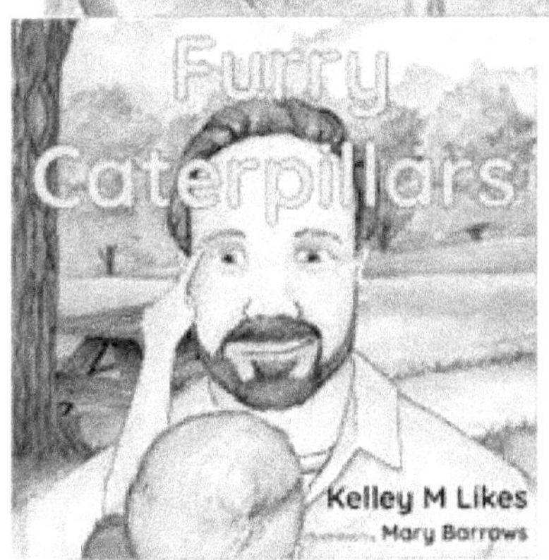
Furry
Caterpillars
Kelley M Likes
Mary Barrows

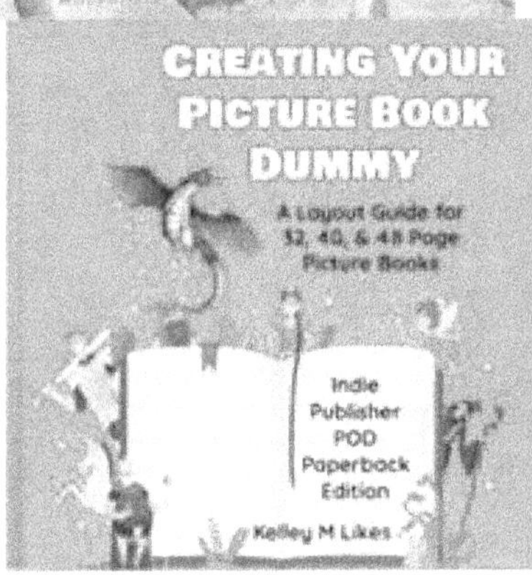
CREATING YOUR
PICTURE BOOK
DUMMY
A Layout Guide for
32, 40, & 48 Page
Picture Books
Indie
Publisher
POD
Paperback
Edition
Kelley M Likes

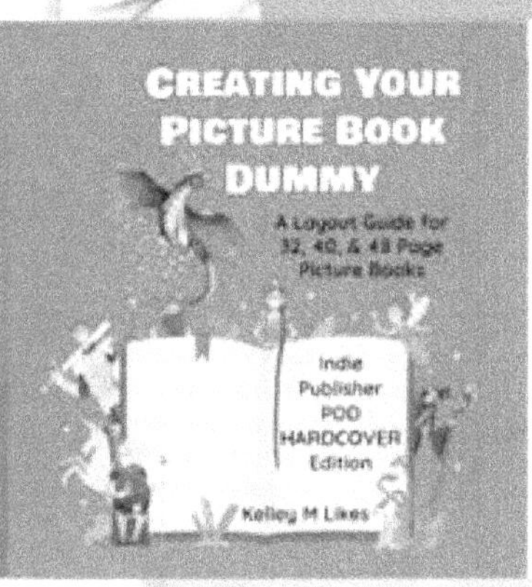
CREATING YOUR
PICTURE BOOK
DUMMY
A Layout Guide for
32, 40, & 48 Page
Picture Books
Indie
Publisher
POD
HARDCOVER
Edition
Kelley M Likes

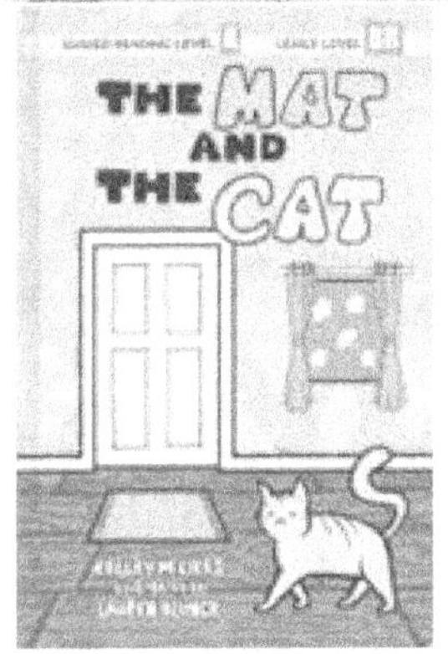
THE MAT
AND
THE CAT

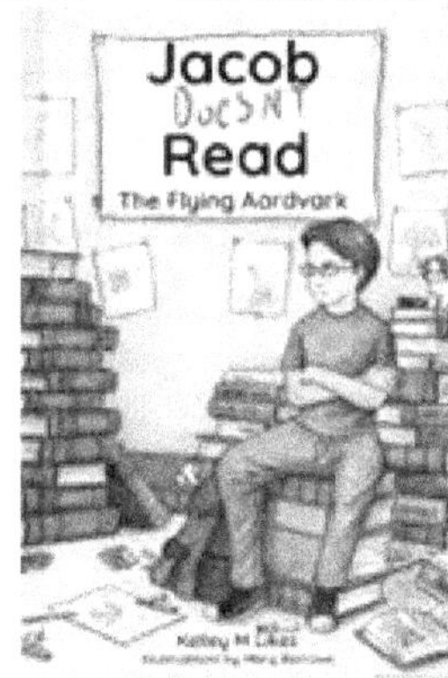
Jacob
DoeSN'T
Read
The Flying Aardvark
Kelley M Likes
Illustrated by Mary Barrows

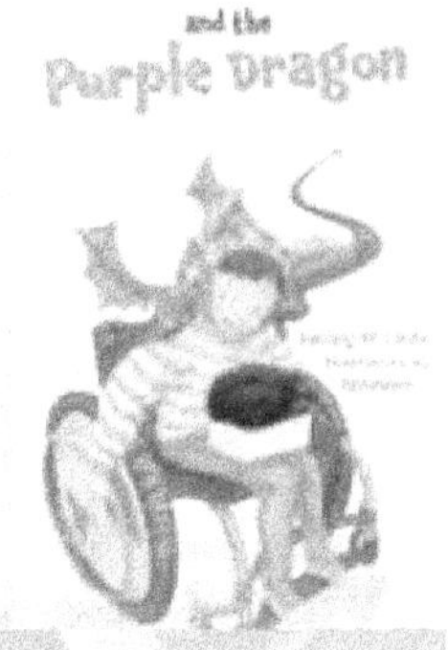
Ben Wise
and the
Purple Dragon

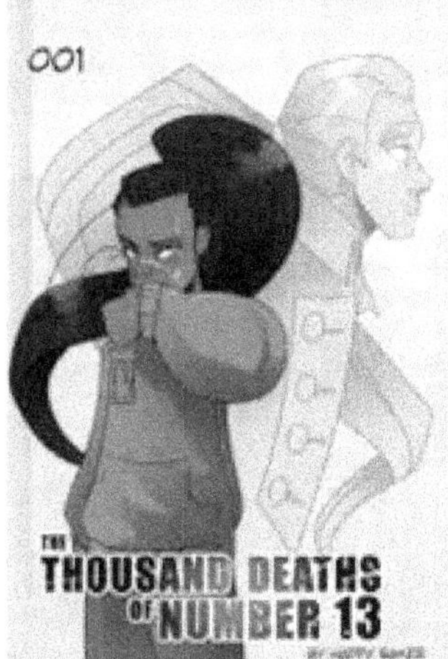
001
THE
THOUSAND DEATHS
OF
NUMBER 13
BY HARRY BAKER

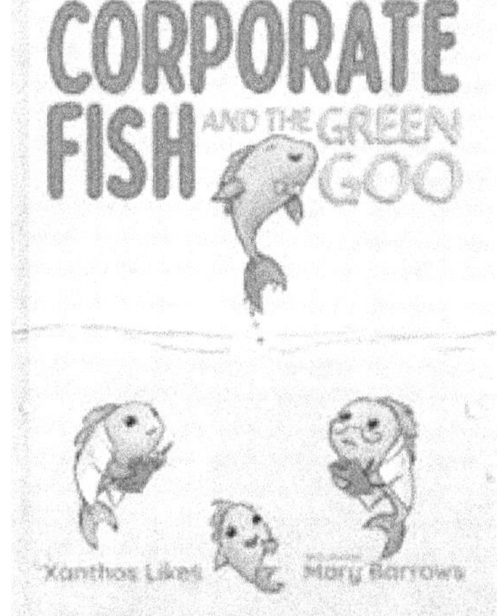
CORPORATE
FISH AND THE GREEN
GOO
Xanthos Likes
Mary Barrows

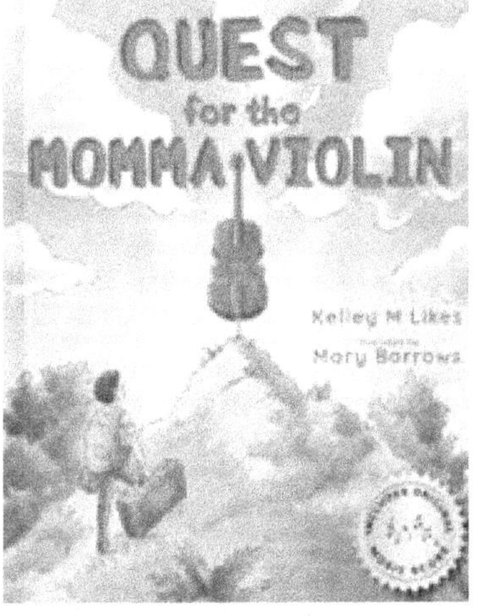
QUEST
for the
MOMMA VIOLIN
Kelley M Likes
Mary Barrows

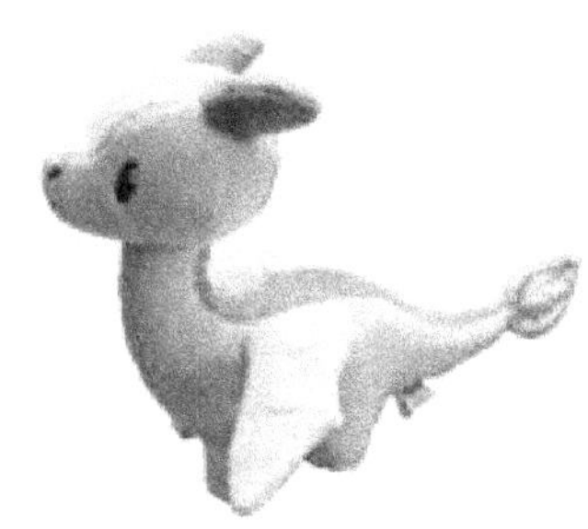